Finding
THE WAY

A Journey Through Abuse, Therapeutic Brilliance and Blunders, to Healing

Denise Stewart

ISBN 1-58169-184-X
For Worldwide Distribution
Printed in the U.S.A.

Gazelle Press
P.O. Box 191540 • Mobile, AL 36619
800-367-8203

TABLE OF CONTENTS

ACKNOWLEDGMENTS

First and foremost, I give thanks to the Lord God Almighty who delivers us out of darkness and into His light. Ephesians 5: 8-17.

Thanks to each and every one of you who have been a part of my life and have loved me in your own special ways. You will remain in my heart forever because I love you. May God bless you and keep you in Jesus name and to His Glory. Amen.

To my husband: It has been 27 years! We have been through so much. I would not want to have gone through what we have with anyone else. One thing we have learned is how to always pull through together, even during those times when we felt we were all alone. Thank you for trying to keep God first, and for making room for me to try to do the same. Thank you for being the best Dad to Julie and Heather. We have much to be thankful for. I love you forever.

To our daughters: I am sorry that this writing (and all that it represents) has taken so much of my time. In some indescribable way; this is all for you in an attempt to break cycles, to make your lives a little brighter at some level, to guide and encourage you and to always let you know that I have deeply loved you. The two of you are in my heart always; no matter what, seek and keep God in the center of yours. God will always have a plan and purpose specifically designed for each of you. He is the bottom line of what pure love is for you. His love is far greater than mine and far more accurate to what you need in this playground and battlefield that we live in. Still, please know that I love you the best that I can from the bottom of my heart forever.

Thank you, Skylar and Nathan for the overflowing joy

you bring to me just by being. Thanks also to your Daddy and Mommy for bringing you into my life. You are each definitely a special gift from God. Grandma loves you and will always have plenty of kisses and hugs for both of you.

Mom, thank you for believing in me. While I express difficult things in this book for the purpose of helping myself and others, I look back at all of the loving ways you have made imprints upon who I am. Beyond the basic care of mother to child, I cherish our talks, our many laughs, our memories and all of the times that you have provided extra kindnesses. I thank God that He has given me you as my mother, and you are in my heart forever. Through all things, we stand. I love you.

Much love and thanks to the friends who kindly read my preliminary manuscript. Thank you for your willingness to be involved, for your care and for your encouragement. Thanks Karen and Randi for your support of me throughout these years, for being willing to take a look at life the way I see it, for holding me at the depths that I have shared my heart, and for wanting to see my dreams come true. Donna, thank you also for reading some of my more finished work and for believing and encouraging me that God's best for me is yet to come. Carney, Christ's love is unfailing. I agree with you in prayer: May God use this writing to heal the brokenhearted, set the captives free and to bring glory to His Holy Name. May God's blessing be upon each of you, in Jesus' name I pray. Amen.

I am pleased to be able to thank my literary agent and coach from Manuscript Placement Service, Keith, for his care in reviewing my manuscript and offering me helpful feedback. I am also delighted to thank my publisher, Brian, and senior editor, Kathy, from Genesis Communications, Inc. Thank you both for the impressive book cover, editing and sensitivity to the content of *Finding the Way*. As I have worked with the three of you, I have felt the security of your faith and have valued the sense of covering that I have experienced. Thank you and God bless you in all your future endeavors.

Praise God for all who have impacted me with the blessings of their spiritual lives and commitment to the Father. There have been far too many to name whose influential lives have consistently stood for Jesus Christ. I think of friends, family, pastors, and Sunday school teachers who have never drifted from the path of the Holy Spirit as He has led them into a life of service, making lasting impressions of God's love upon His children.

I specifically thank my Grandma (December 12, 1915-December 20, 2004). Grandma heard a message by Kathryn Kuhlman over a half a century ago that took her to her knees. Thank God that Grandma spent 54 years of her lifetime both on her knees and standing before her Lord and Savior. Through the strength she sought and received from God, Grandma endured opposition, displayed all of the fruits of the Spirit, and continued to love and guide us and remain our rock of Gibraltar. Yet, she would decline that she ever did a thing as Grandma gave God all of the glory. I pray that in the land of Glory she will see the fruits of her labor as her family surrounds her there. I know that our salvation has been the greatest desire of Grandma's heart. May our family cling to God's Word, believe in Him, and claim His victory. In the name of Jesus Christ, the Risen Savior. Amen.

Lay hold of my words with all your heart; keep my commands and you will live. Get wisdom, get understanding, . . . Do not forsake wisdom, and she will protect you; love her and she will watch over you. . . .Though it cost all you have, get understanding. Esteem her, and she will exalt you; embrace her, and she will honor you. She will set a garland of grace on your head and present you with a crown of splendor. . . .Hold on to instruction, do not let it go; guard it well, for it is your life. Do not set foot on the path of the wicked or walk in the way of evil men. Avoid it, do not travel on it; turn from it and go on your way (Proverbs 4: 4-15 LAB).

Jesus replied, If anyone loves me, he will obey my teaching (John 14:23a).

. . .I am the way and the truth and the life. No one comes to the Father except through me (John 14: 6).

Jesus, I love you. May His Word come alive in us. In Jesus' name. Amen.

INTRODUCTION

Often in my prayers, I ask God to tell me His story. I want to know the details in whatever ways He wants to share His life with me. I want to receive His story in a way that I need or can identify with at the moment when I ask. Sometimes there is a hunger deep inside of me to know Jesus in a way that touches right where I am hurting and moves me through my healing process. His story may reflect His pain, His joy, His strength, His suffering or whatever I need. In the same way, I offer my story to you.

Recently, my brother died at the age of 38. The impact of his death is not fully known to me nor has the impact of his life been fully realized. One reflection I have had is that if I knew I was leaving here tomorrow, one of my greatest regrets would be unspoken words with others. Yet, communication in relationship can be so hard. My struggle with overcoming childhood sexual abuse has been both difficult to contain and difficult to share. The sensitivity of this moment, my brother's death, leaves me yet with other questions about sharing such personal information—information that touches more lives than simply my own. This information touches the lives of family whom I love and feel deeply bonded to. It is difficult to weigh what is best as I desire to provide some unspoken words and allow God to use me as a vessel in providing His healing touch in other people's lives. I hear the voices of those who have similar shared experiences crying out to me to speak the words and finish the sentences.

In this writing, I surrender trying to be in control of such a task of weighing the potential fruit, and perhaps the pain, of my words. Instead, I ask God to help me tell my story in a way that touches lives and moves all of us to a closer relationship with Him and to deeper and greater levels of healing.

One part of Jesus' story is that He came to heal the brokenhearted. Maybe it is time to let Him heal some of the brokenhearted through these pages. Perhaps there is even a greater picture than the one I see. So, I walk in faith and cry out to God to help me tell my story in a way that comes from His heart, intertwining His story with mine. I ask Him to allow these stories to momentarily mingle with yours, and I ask the Holy Spirit to perform miracles of healing in each of us. May the words used be for this time as we temporarily join together in the journey of our lives.

The concept of time is vague in the framework of healing. It encompasses a meeting of common experiences, yet varies in each of our lives with all of eternity. Our spiritual journey often moves forward when we reach deep inside and bring to light those things which have hindered our growth. It is at that point when the Holy Spirit offers us counsel, insight, wisdom, healing, wholeness, and deliverance. There is one level allowing a sequence of events to evolve throughout these pages such as that described in the "Contents" section of this book. There is yet another level that is an opening of layers where a sequence of events exists only in God's framework of time. I recommend that you "lean not unto your own understanding" in this matter. Whether in your experience or mine, simply allow the story of life to unfold as it does. How it begins, evolves, and ends "only God knows," and "only time will tell." For now, this is my story.

Considering the personal subject matter of this book, balancing the authenticity of experience with spiritual integrity has been a challenge—hopefully one with successful results. Originally, the writings happened because I needed them. While protecting the genuineness of my journey for a greater cause, I have also had to risk exposing myself in ways that are generally private and extremely self-protective. My hope is that my insights and experiences will serve to prove useful to you. I also hope that this writing will be one that you can interact with. Ask the questions you need to ask as they apply to your life or the life of a loved one. Seek and find the way for you.

These may or may not be the writings that will minister to you. You see, it is my soul that decorates the pages of this story that I am about to put down on paper. Keep in touch with your feelings and reach out to others if you need help. You may even need to let go of the things you see by putting them away. Or, you may stay with me on the journey of the truth that sets me as free as I can be for now. If you like, we can walk together in places you cannot comprehend while risking the challenge of trying in your efforts to love. . .to love yourself and to love someone different from you. Grow to care, and care to grow.

There is only one condition in choosing to turn the pages that you hold in your hands: "Love one another as He has first loved you." We are all God's children; the evildoers and the saints—and the evil-doing saints. So, "ye without sin cast the first stone" and ye with sin "judge not lest ye be judged." Know that God is God, so that when times are tough and the places deep within you ache beyond your ability to describe the pain—seek the "peace that passeth beyond all understanding" and "be still" God loves you. Let it in. . .

—Denise Stewart, 2005

CHAPTER ONE

Once or So Upon a Time

Mom and Dad are fighting again. I am so scared that I can't breathe. I wonder when it will end, how it will end, what I can do, and who will still be alive. I hear the anger building; I am very still. Tension holds me in place like invisible walls around me. I can't move; I can't hide. My fear becomes even greater as my father pounds the table. I watch the dishes fly and cringe when I hear them break. It is as if an angry lion is roaring and frantically pacing as it anticipates an attack on its prey. My mother is helpless. The words that she uses in defense only make the lion more anxious. My eyes see him attack. She runs. She is gone.

I watch my father. I wish I could hide. I wonder how I can please him. My hands, like those of a robot, begin to clean up the glass. The glass cuts them, but I am so frozen with fear that I don't feel the pain. Who will help me?

My father walks out of the kitchen, then back in again. He tells me to go and find my mother. Relieved, I run out the door without even grabbing a coat. Through the snow I trudge alone and feel comfort in the cold silence of the night. I finally find my mother being comforted by a friend. She must have hugged me; I don't know. They talk about divorce. I pray she goes through with it this time before it's too late. I don't want to accept the fact that she might not.

Suddenly, the shock wears off and I begin to cry. My comfort is a tissue given to me through the efforts of my mother's friend. I am touched that she reached out to me and I gain strength from it. My mother wants to go out with her friend. I want her to feel better. I assure her it's okay. I feel so alone as I look around. Once again, she is gone.

It is New Year's Eve. Happy New Year Mom and Dad. Happy New Year, Denise.

And so began 1974. I wanted to please my dad—to me it felt like survival—but I also wanted my parents to divorce. The ongoing stress was incredibly high and so thick in the air that I vividly remember the difficulty I had in breathing even now. I didn't know it then, but I was angry for many years that my mom did not protect me. I set my needs aside, hoping not to add complications to her life so that she could free us from my dad's maniacal tantrums. During 1974 my parents' indecision about getting a divorce led to a car chase in which my dad threatened to kill my mom. Then she moved in with my grandma for about two weeks, and I smuggled out my youngest brother to my mom when my dad was not home. I feared being caught, but the worst punishment of all was that my dad sexually abused me.

It was the classic case of a daughter trying to protect her mom. I tried to please and make peace with Dad, but sensed that he felt powerless. His control over my body and me seemed to make him feel in control of the entire situation. I went to school pretending everything was normal. On the inside, I felt withdrawn and confused about what I could do to stop the abuse. What could I do? Would my dad kill my mom if I told her? The shame that belonged to my dad became my possession more fully with each of his invasions upon me. What did I do? I was an obedient child, but my mind was continually trying to cope with what was way over my head. I tried in several ways to get him to stop, from saying "no" to writing him a letter. I tried to figure out who I could trust to tell. I was so ashamed.

Five months later, it no longer mattered if I died or my father killed my family. I could not hold it in any longer and told my mom. That same day, my mom told me of her long-time affair with a family friend. We had shared our secrets. My mother confronted my dad. No one died, except that I had lost my dad since I could never feel safe with him again. My mom took me out on dates with her—no longer able to leave me in the hands of my dad.

Life went on. I married the year of my high school graduation (two weeks after my 18th birthday). With whatever turmoil I felt about my childhood, I was extremely thankful for my husband and for my daughters who were both born prior to my 22nd birthday. My parents finally got their divorce (at my father's request three months after my wedding). My father died when I was 22. He left without resolution between us. Being gone forever was his cruelest trick of all. What my dad also left me with was the resulting anger. I needed help in dealing with the anger, and I wrote . . .

Urgent Birth

From within myself there is a volcanic urge. This erupting force causes a desire in me to express myself. Express what, I ask with pen and paper waiting impatiently for some answers—waiting for some organized, sensible understanding. Express what, I ask with a barely controllable emotion pushing and pulling at me.

It is an emotion comparable to a woman far into labor. It is the child pushing to exit and ready to enter the next phase of life. It is the child growing beyond its present boundaries. It is the woman—using her entire mind, soul, and body—desperately working to expel what is within. This emotion is an urgency to deliver what can no longer possibly be contained.

Child, there you are cramped within your small appointed space—your mother's womb. You are pushed and pulled by other forces as you struggle for birth. You want to get on with life. You strive to be free—to take your own first breath.

Innocent child, not yet touched by adult fears and confusion. Curious child with an open uncluttered mind, thriving to understand, to learn, to grow, to know everything. Naïve child, trusting in and dependent on the perfect parents and all the other grownup people who surely know everything.

Child, two decades later, you are now an adult yourself. Although outside the womb, you are still cramped in your small-appointed space. You are still being pushed and pulled by outside forces. You are still trying to grow, still trying to be free. Trapped more than ever, you struggle. Life is more exhausting, and you have grown weaker.

Oh child, where have you gone? Aren't you going to dance? Aren't you going to sing? Two decades later and yes the urge is great! Again I ask myself what I am compelled to express. Intensely I search and somehow I can only conceive of one answer.

From within myself, the adult—now also the mother—there is a volcanic urge to express, to release, to deliver the child within who still wants to dance...the child who still wants to sing...the child who still wants to know everything...the child who still wants to be free. The child who is myself—the growing child—the adult me. (August 1, 1984)

So, what could I do with all this emotion? At that time I managed drugstores. One of my employees began telling me about a radio talk show she listened to. I found the radio station, I listened, and I called.

Phone Calls (part one) 1984

One moment merged into the next. Each experience was a prerequisite to the following. Life's motion continued flowing like a river, sometimes angrily, along its chosen path. Yet the moments and the experiences became one as the woman sat on her bed in quiet desperation and fearfully waited for a voice to answer her call. The woman waited in anticipation; she was determined to be heard. The telephone rang again and again as though it too was pleading for help and waiting for an answer. . .pause . . .help. . .pause. . .help.. .pause. . . .Finally, a stranger's voice answered and connected the anxious woman to the radio talk show host.

The woman allowed the words that had been sporadically dancing in her head to exit her mouth in a cool, calm, and collected voice. Before all of the radio station listeners, she said . . .the woman said. . .I said. . .my father involved me in incest when I was 14, and I feel like I want to ask you a question, but I don't know what it is. The questions became easy for her as she asked them of me. Among her questions, she asked about my marriage, my relationship with my father, my mother, my small daughters, and myself.

Blinded by my denial and my perfect family fantasies, I told her that my father had died the previous year. She responded, "How dare he die!" She talked about how some women who have been involved in incest play tough and suggested that I get into group counseling "to tie up some loose ends." She was warm and caring and her words touched me as though she knew places in my heart that I could not see. Her words remained in my mind.

Beneath my "Brady Bunch" disguise and my "all is well" replies, I felt miserable. The weight of the world seemed to be upon me. I thought there was no one to see beneath my pride and illusion. No one knew I was faking it through my life, not even me. No one helped, or perhaps I wouldn't let them until I couldn't run from myself anymore. . .until I was forced to face the pain and the shame. . .until I risked one small step of faith. . .until I called someone who knew from out of her own experiences.

At this time, I still really did not know how to follow through and get the help I needed. The truth is that I hated living so far from my hometown area. My dad had died, and so had my nephew, and all I wanted was to go home and be near my family. When I called the radio station, I was also working a 48-plus hours per week job, taking a computer class at the nearby college, and was busy with family and friends. My daughters were ages 2 and 4, and obviously needed much of my care. Also, whatever was going on for my mom was bringing out lots of my "where are you, mom" hurt and anger. I begged my mother to drive the approximately 12 hours to spend time with us, to see our first home, and to share in our lives there. I needed her. I offered to pay her way and give her access to my phone to keep in touch with her friends for a week or two. My mother did not come. When my family moved five hours away from my mother, she still did not come. My dad was dead; and, my mom did not come to visit me for six or seven years until I moved back to my hometown area. I felt abandoned and rejected during those years. My mother and I had some arguments. I was hurting; although to admit those words was difficult. As for my Dad. . .

Crazy Like Me

I remember watching my father suddenly tear the shirt from his body and chase my mother out of the house. I felt terrorized and I decided I would never grow up crazy like my father. I would not slam boards into the shins of a young boy, break crutches over a woman, or strangle a teenager's throat black and blue. No, I would not rip anyone's hair out, cut them with belts, throw them across rooms, hold them by their feet and bounce their heads off the floor. No way would I slap them, punch them, kick them, or verbally destroy them. Huh uh, not me. I would never molest anyone or be crazy in any way like he was. No way, no way! But, sometimes, just sometimes I would like to break dishes, slap someone or chase them out of the house. Sometimes, I would like to scream out, strike out, and do all of the things he did, but I would not. However, maybe I could be crazy enough to throw a book, pound a chair, and swing my arms towards someone and hold them tightly as I fall against them and cry like a child. Maybe I could be a little crazy— not like my father, but crazy—like me.

> Family violence kills as many women every five years as the total number of Americans who died in the Vietnam War. —*American Medical Association*

Despite everything I have experienced or heard about, the above statistic stuns me. I continue to be dismayed at the number of people who look into each other's eyes and even make oaths of love before God and yet murder their spouses and children. Sometimes people do things to one another that cause total outrage, but outrage does not have to kill to be expressed. I wrote something during a time when I was feeling pure rage. I have chosen not to include it with the rest because I do not believe sharing this particular writing will serve any purpose. Nonetheless, I think writing it for myself at the time was valuable.

To take a moment to focus on the rage that people experience and the choices of how to handle their anger is also important. My God, how we need to feel love in these dark places within us. Wounding and killing another is not going to help us. We need each other. I need you here in this place of pain that burns the fires of hell from within me. I need your love and the love of others here in this place where I have expressed myself so violently. We destroy one another verbally, trying to have some sense of power, or take back some sense of ourselves when all we need is love.

> Heavenly Father, hold me in your arms. I need to feel your mercy, your grace, and your light in my darkness. I do not need to harm anyone, Lord. I just need to cry for the evil done in this world, say something about it, release the anger to you through the tears of my prayer, and rest. I am so sorry when I am hurtful to others. Help me to forgive so that I will be forgiven. Help me to stop, take a breath, and rest peacefully in your arms. In Jesus' name I pray. Amen.

Permission To Be Loved

"I am sorry," I said in a soft voice from deep within. Then, I cried out, "I'm sorry! I'm sorry! I'm sorry!"

Another voice asserted, "You have nothing to be ashamed of."

With thoughts of my father, I responded, "I couldn't help him."

She said, "It wasn't your place to help him."

"I loved him!" I cried.

Nurturing, yet with strength in her voice the woman said, "You loved him and you tried. You did the best that you could, now allow yourself that. He had to do it and he didn't know how. It is not your fault! You were a good girl, a beautiful, wonderful girl. He had to help himself, and he didn't know how. He had to leave to find out how. He is where he is happiest now. Now, he is getting the help he needs." Lovingly, my friend ordered, "Now, you start helping yourself."

Just then, the tape player we were recording with clicked off—further emphasizing her final words, "Now, you start helping yourself. . .now, you start helping yourself. . .now, you. . . ." Thank you, my friend.

The following writing is about a mother and daughter who lived clinging to one another as if both were out in the middle of the ocean somewhere. Both were struggling to swim, but figuratively drowning one another instead. As both seek to grab onto the father/husband for all of their needs, he strikes out in his own sense of powerlessness and self-preservation.

Our Bermuda Triangle

For too long we gave our all to love the man—
You in search of love, approval, and a male to please,
    and me in search of my daddy's girl fantasy.
Our past was subtly competitive, painfully repetitive,

Yet, we held tightly to our female creed,
  as we clung together out of helpless need.

In our own ways we tried, we cried,
While parts of us passively died;
Until the man born powerless to complete us,
Who in powerlessness often seemed alive only to de-
feat us, Passed away.

Separately we search to replace
  the father, the martyr, the man.
Unconsciously, we proudly manipulate
Until we finally fearfully face
And learn to spiritually fill our own space
With the love and power we regained
  from when we gave our all to love the man.

In our own ways we'll try, and we'll still cry;
But sometimes we'll fly.
While the man born powerless to complete us,
Who lived, never actually intending to defeat us,
Flies away.

Filling the Void

After my dad died, my mother remained on and off involved
in her relationship with the longtime family friend. Fifteen
years later, they moved in with one another. As for me, I
fought for more support from my husband, my first therapist, my personal growth workshops, my psychology
courses, my prayer life, my friends, and my church. My goal
was to have the void in me filled somehow. While completing the previous sentence, I received a phone call from

someone who was helping me therapeutically with closure in relationship to both my dad and the first therapist I ever sought help from.

Both relationships had ended abruptly and unfinished. I needed to stop and cry because loss still touches me deeply and this woman cared enough to respond when I reached out to her. She said, "Denise, I got your letter, and I hear you. . . ." The act of responding back is parallel to having communion with God and all that is good, with the exception that God is always there and He never hangs up the phone as we do. If you, as a survivor, have not known how to ask for or receive such love, find the courage to simply ask for whatever small thing that the person (within their boundaries) can reasonably give to you (i.e. A two minute phone call, a hug, an encouraging word, a moment of silence together, a prayer). Also, remember that people can only love in the ways that they know how. Please do not hurt yourself by asking someone over and over again for something they cannot provide. Seek the ones capable of loving in the ways you need loved.

I can still remember the amazing joy of someone suddenly and gently reaching out and rubbing my back as she held me in her arms while I wept. She was the first person I had let see the overwhelming feelings I had as I spoke of the sexual abuse. I remember playing with a Kermit the frog hand puppet as I talked until the weight of the emotion prevented me from talking anymore. Kermit and I sort of slumped over together. This caring woman swiftly moved beside me and repeated the rubbing that I had been doing on Kermit's back onto my back. Now, I smile because I picture her petite frame in her button down sweater watching me talk that day and really listening. I remember how I felt the light of her love. Together, we opened the door for me to have the right and the ability to slowly let a moment of love into this area of my life. God used her to plant a seed that would help me grow to feel safe, entitled and deserving of the comfort I needed. Thank God who is my Comforter and my Provider.

As for "Our Bermuda Triangle" in relationship to my history, the abuse and chaos that occurred between mother, father, and daughter has a societal context. Women did not have economical opportunities and laws were different up until the 80s. Much support for women and children facing domestic violence was just being pioneered. The establishment of agencies (to provide shelters for those fearful for their lives and without the financial and educational resources to reside independently and safely) was new.

Even now, there are still too many women experiencing traumatic family lives who need to be educated and risk change in the midst of their vulnerability and feeling of powerlessness. If you are in such a relationship, reach out to others who are in healthy loving relationships. We all need one another. We need support from outside sources.

It takes prayer for God to bring about transformation and healing. So if you are banging your head against the wall or having it banged against the wall for you, surrender your situation to God and please call a hotline, or go to a shelter or to a family member or friend's home that can offer you support and safety. You have resources. Expend your energy to meet your needs in a healthy way. Make enough space to reassess the situation and find the objectivity to truly determine what God's plans are for you and what is in the best interest of all. I believe that we all have the opportunity to live together as healthier family units. Sometimes, things must appear worse in this life before they get better or healed. For now, take a deep breath and rest awhile within the arms of Jesus and of savored memories from those who have touched your hearts with kindness and care.

Take a moment to think of those who have deeply touched your life even in small ways and then open your heart with joy and thanksgiving. Tears are welcome as well. Write their names or speak aloud from your heart in thanksgiving for them and for the ways they have touched your life. Take as much time as you need. Although it is easy to slip into focusing on those who were not there for you when you rightfully needed and expected their love, I encourage you to keep your eyes on those who did arrive just in time to give you a glimmer of love and hope. Embrace and savor this love. It could even be in a passing look from a stranger that has stayed with you. It could be from anyone along the way who has made a difference—large or small. Never underestimate the value and power of just even one small gesture. Receive it and allow yourself to savor all that you are thankful for. Let the impact of that which is good flow through you. It is safe and good to receive God's blessings and His love through others along your way. Trust Him. He will never hurt you.

CHAPTER 2

Incest. . . and The Void

Boundaries: Phone Calls (part 2)

I heard her voice. I heard the beep. I heard my heart pound against the bed. I felt my heart and muscles beat against my chest and legs. I listened and thought she is just a woman and I love her. Why am I so afraid? I prayed. I cried. I felt cold, yet somehow calm. I drank warm tea. I wrote (the words you are reading now). I went to sleep.

The above phone call/answering machine experience was with my first counselor. Thoughts of my relationship with her will resurface throughout these pages as they have throughout these years when I have felt haunted by her, similar to the way that the incest continued to rear its ugly head and steal my life away. This therapist once told me that my "boundaries were way out there somewhere." That was just another thing she said that she never bothered to explain. I had no concrete examples or understanding of what she was talking about. So, what I learned about the term called "boundaries" was from someone whom I felt had held them in her hands, beating me over the head with them. The only way I was able to assimilate what the "teacher" was saying was to first encounter someone who was firm yet gentle, present, and caring enough for me to trust in the midst of painful lessons. What I want to say to you is do not stay with one counselor if it is not helping! Talk about it with God and make choices because He is a loving God and His plan is not to harm you.

I learned this lesson best when I stayed too long in a therapeutic relationship trying to persuade the therapist to hug me when I was talking about painful experiences. I became so depressed that I needed anti-depressants for the first time in my life to help me out of the relationship that served to open my wounds, but left me feeling too vulnerable to share them. Each of our needs for healing is different. I was not going to take someone into the depths of my pain if she could not hold me appropriately when I was hurting. I went into the depths of the pain with my dad touching my body inappropriately and my mother not being someone I felt safe trusting with my emotions. With the body memories involved and the difficulty in feeling comfortable in my own body at times, a therapist courageous, trusting, and compassionate enough to hold me became my boundary for when I again would allow someone to do therapy with me.

Boundaries vary with each relationship. Being flexible

enough to confront various places of the boundary (to appropriately keep the relationship healthy and in harmony) is quite a skill to learn if respect for each individual and their thoughts, feelings, and bodies is not a natural part of what is learned as a member of a healthy family unit. This topic regarding therapists and boundaries is an extremely important one both in the context of sharing my personal experience as well as in representing the voices of painful client/therapist experiences shared with me by many others. One brief example occurred upon my entering college where one professor/therapist lost his job due to his inappropriate and unethical sexual misconduct in his therapeutic practice. I mention the given example simply because it was the first lesson to me of how someone that had taught psychology (within the field that I was choosing to help people), had used his position to hurt them. He was found guilty and dismissed. Other counselors I have heard about have gotten away with similar criminal behaviors. These "professionals" seriously need to seek God's forgiveness and transformation rather than be found guilty in His courtroom.

I add a note to the counselors in this world: Amidst the ethics and cautions you keep with you, I ask that you only open the door of friendship if somewhere along the path of the relationship, you intend to have a friendship rather than a friendly counseling relationship. What is my reason for this statement? Two separate therapists shared with me that their spouses had committed suicide, both during my therapy sessions. As a compassionate person, I cared. Both therapists had opened a door and I responded to one with a hug and to both with a great sense of empathy and a sense of friendship.

A therapist may say that I took on dual roles as I still needed help, and I cared in a reciprocal way that does not work in therapy. If someone is sharing something important, I have to care. My job is to love my neighbor as myself—no qualifiers, no regrets. I guess that what I am saying overall is that even therapeutic relationships can unproductively create further psychological pain. Just because someone is a therapist does not mean he or she possesses the ability to help in various areas, such as the dynamics of incest. Several years after being away from my first therapist, I wrote her a letter that begins like this:

Dear _____:

I woke up tearfully wondering if you had meant to reinforce the message in my heart that I am bad and valueless. The message hurts and gentleness is most healing. Fear rejects and hurts people. I'm sorry for mine, but must be gentle with myself for I know the suffering from which it originates. I wish that our relationship had ended more gently. . . .

Is this letter a bit of "transference"? Sure. My dad died when our relationship had been unresolved. Still, the relationship with the therapist could have ended more gently. In the second therapeutic relationship, I left feeling ashamed of my neediness for a hug. I wondered if the intention was for me to leave the relationship feeling undeserving to the point of wanting to shrink inside of myself and never again risk reaching out for help.

Based on a True Story

"What does it feel like?" she asks. "I don't need to know the details of the incest, but I think it would be helpful to express the feelings." I answer, "Will you hold me?" She says, "No." I say, "Do you love me?" She says, "What does love have to do with it?" Knowing that to speak the words aloud will not matter (having already tried), I think very loudly to myself, "Everything," and I go away.

Way away, deep within myself, tears pour from my eyes. I feel so alone in my pain. I turn from person to person only to bang my head on walls—the walls of confinement. Wearing down; I turn sporadically, frantically, awkwardly. I am afraid that someone will hurt me again. I warn the weary guard of my heart, "Watch out."

"I'll get help," I tell myself. Where? When? Who? Reaching, getting closer, never touching—like the days of the incest. Checklist: Teacher? No. Pastor? No. Guidance Counselor? No. Church? No. Grandma? No. Neighbor? No. Mother? No. No. No! No one could protect me from the murderer of my sanity, my reality, my security, my joy, and my serenity.

The original questions revisited: "What does it feel like?" "What does love have to do with anything?"

"Everything," I say, as I wander away in pain.

Simply Love

Had it simply been:
    A needy hunger attachment,
    A desire to be special,

A misunderstanding of boundaries,
Or a disagreement of logic,
My life would feel so much lighter.
Had it simply been:
An inability to help each other through,
Four arms around two bodies,
Hours in a lifetime. . .
Or the distribution thereof,
My life would feel so much lighter.

But, what it was and is. . .is simply love.
And when two hearts meet again,
My life will feel so much lighter.
I miss you.

Describing incest and expressing buried emotion is usually as vital as a volcano that needs to erupt or a baby that needs to be born. The articulation of such expression is not always graceful or expressed in polite language. Writing has helped me release buried words and emotions. Other helpful forms of anger management have been to talk to someone (especially God); to write down my thoughts and feelings, then bury, shred or burn them surrendering them to God; to cry out or beat on a pillow to help bring forth the tears; or to do some form of physical exercise (i.e., walking, running, singing, passing a baseball, playing volleyball, sled riding, skiing). As I work out what has held me captive through releasing what I have held captive and asking God to take them, I have less need for finding other ways to release the anger and cancerous thoughts. If you happen to be committing the crime that I am describing, God sees everything and vengeance is His. Praise God for He is a just God in wrath as well as in grace. Turn away from your sin and turn to Him.

Seek His forgiveness and receive His grace.

Incest hurts so much! It is so ugly and disgusting! This incredible void is not always instantly healed through the miracles of Christ. I believe wholeheartedly in the Bible verse; Matthew 9:22 (LAB). "Jesus turned and saw her. 'Take heart, daughter,' he said, 'your faith has healed you.'" I believed all along in the healing of my heart. It just did not happen so instantly. If you hear incest being expressed, look beyond the ugly to the description of events and feelings.

Analyze the mixed messages I received from my earthly and heavenly fathers. Imagine how hard it is to sort out all of the messages when childhood has not provided a solid foundation for a spiritual belief system. Take a look at the challenge we have been given to love one another and that I have been given to love my dad who violated my body.

How much of a struggle is it for you to hear my story and love me? Therein lies one of the burdens and additional causes of suffering for a survivor trying to exist in the world of those who have not had to suffer this way. It is much more of a struggle for me to actually forgive and love having lived through the experience. What are your expectations of yourself? What expectations do you have of me in comparison to you? I have my own expectation of myself to forgive, love, and heal. I have taken on the expectation that Jesus has for me in His greatest commandment. Still, incest continues every day to children all around us and this is not okay. Pain continues. Incest is very ugly, but I am not ugly.

I am not just speaking on behalf of my experience. I am advocating right this minute on behalf of powerless and voiceless children that you may even know and love. God, please help, comfort, and protect the children! To my readers, please take the time right now to offer a prayer to God for the children in such sexual, emotional, and physical abuse situations presently occurring around the world, in your cities, in your neighborhoods, and even in your churches. Especially pray for the children of those who were to have served as loving parents, role models, and representatives of God in the children's young lives but have instead committed travesty on them. God hears your prayers; He is good and loving, and desires to deliver and heal His children. Thank God that He has not forgotten them or any one of us even when everything seems hopeless.

I know of little children who had been placed in foster homes due to sexual abuse in their natural family. A couple of foster parents described the disgust they felt toward them and finally decided they couldn't care for such children. I understand the disgust, but don't misplace it on innocent children—place it on the adult who committed such atrocious behavior. Place it on evil in the world or a society of indulgence or generational cycles of abuse and societal fear and indifference. Please don't blame the child for being vulnerable, helpless, and exposed to a perversion that is so far beyond them to comprehend let alone prevent.

I remember being in so much pain and fear that I would hyperventilate every time I got too close to talking about the abuse I experienced. When I was in the midst of hyperventilating, my hands became stiff and distorted from the lack of oxygen. It would take awhile before I could move my fingers. This happened to me when I was with my second therapist. I waited until I was fairly calm and my hands weren't so freaky looking, then I asked my counselor to hold my hands. She wouldn't. Her explanation was that my dad sexually abused me and my mom was not available to hold me when I hurt, so she did not want to confuse me. I think she was confused.

In thinking about this counselor and the first counselor I had ever reached out to, I know there was a darkness inside of me where I felt so helpless. In looking for the light, the search was never quite right. From that feeling of darkness once came:

Curdled Love

Tiny fingers and toes, not yet ready to stand
    let alone stand alone
Politely cry out with fear, or rather with
    abandonment's life possessing panic

Prop the bottle and out she goes
    closing the door behind.
Tiny mouth grasps the hard plastic nipple
    trying to make it enough.

Her broken spirit absorbs the large room's emptiness
    along with each swallow of warm milk.
Warm milk given as love,
But the tiny mind never grasps the symbolism
    enough to stop longing for the bottle propper's
    flesh.
Holding no one within the depths of a desperate
    heart, she holds down the spoiling curdled love.
The still needy woman cries out pitifully
    for crumbs defined as socially appropriate adult

care. Candy, cakes, and cookies become
    the preferred brand of hard, plastic nipple milk.

Grown up fingers and toes pray
    "God, fill my soul with anything but emptiness."
She takes what she can, sometimes panics,
    and always stomachs abandonment's vomit.

Her life becomes a book of longing and
    "how to" strategies of an empty soul
Struggling to cope with life's expectations
    and when tastes of mother love appear,
Her greatest fear becomes rejection
    from her nauseous hurling of curdled love
    turned bile.

Suddenly, from somewhere within my being, a deep compassion springs into my heart. While focusing on the above words, a visual of the second counselor came to mind. Even though she was no longer my counselor at the time of my writing, I saw myself staring into her eyes where I could see compassion. Even now, I feel the compassion within my heart for her. A lot of compassion is required to love and forgive. A lot of forgiveness is required to take in the love in her eyes, fill the emptiness, and bring light to the darkness—a light that only the presence of Christ, the Risen Savior, can create. While believing that Jesus could replace His divinity back into the crevices of my life, I begged for His presence and healing. Opening my heart so fully to Him, Jesus filled me with love and compassion as He opened my eyes to see the same in hers.

I speak about mother's love often with regard to my mom. It is a common area of emotional anguish for incest survivors.

But mostly, I think I long for the ability to more freely allow others into those dark places that we all face in our lives. It is so difficult for me to share my tears and trustingly expect to receive comfort. I think of this sense of emotional deprivation as somehow perpetuating a void that society doesn't understand. Frustrated and feeling our own neediness, we hurl this curdled love and get angry when it isn't satisfying for others or satisfied within us. Fearfully, we hurt one another. We stop trusting, not feeling able to take any more pain upon us. We close up, not wanting to hurt or be hurt. We hold out our open hand toward another because our hearts need loved so much. Then, with the slightest abruptness of action on the part of the other that reminds us that we might get hurt again, we snatch our hand back. We close up. . .or risk to open once again. . . .

Spiritual Reflections

I reached for you today. I felt confused when I thought you were reaching too, yet somehow we couldn't touch.

I wondered if I hadn't been open enough. Maybe I was only wishing that we had reached toward each other. Perhaps you didn't even want my touch. Why was it that I wanted yours?

In search of my answers, I went inside of myself to touch you. I asked to quietly look into your eyes. As the moment passed, our breathing matched in peaceful rhythm. There were no words, yet there was conversation.

I watched the garments that clothe our hearts, that

block our vision and stand between us. I saw them as they softened and fell away. It was at that moment that our spirits touched.

Then, words came to me and I dared to share them with you. I said, "You are not all that I thought you were, but when I open my heart, I am able to see that you are so much more than I thought."

I paused for a while to understand these words. With the same feeling of spiritual unity, I gave the words to myself. I said, "I am not all that I thought I was, but when I open my heart I am able to see that I am so much more than I thought."

Today, I reached for you; instead, I touched me. When I opened my heart, I saw even more than you and me. I saw God. I saw the God that surrounds us and flows through us. I not only saw God, but I felt His touch.

Our Father, which art in heaven. Hallowed be Thy name. Thy kingdom come. Thy will be done. On earth as it is in heaven. Give us this day our daily bread and forgive us our debts as we forgive our debtors. And, lead us not into temptation, but deliver us from evil, for Thine is the kingdom, and the power, and the glory forever. Amen.

The Lord's Prayer comforts me. The Holy Spirit comes upon me. Thank you, Heavenly Father, for the gifts you have given. I receive and go to sleep allowing His love to pour through me.

CHAPTER 3

Plea For Closure

Earlier I wrote of a phone call from a group counselor that came in the midst of my Bermuda Triangle discussion. Closure with the survivor's group I had been attending triggered the desire to have a proper closure with my first therapist. Follow-up work with the therapist from the group, whose call had been so heartwarming, had been my vehicle to cope with this hurt that I had been feeling.

A night came when I cried until the sun came up. My stereo played songs from a Christian singer, Tammy Trent, whose song acknowledged how I was broken down with the weight of my problems, but to rely on God for strength and grace. Then, Tammy recited the 23rd Psalm:

> *The Lord is my Shepherd, I shall not want. He maketh me to lie down in green pastures. He*

leadeth me beside the still waters. He restoreth my soul. He leadeth me in the paths of righteousness for His name's sake. Yeah though I walk through the valley of the shadow of death, I will fear no evil for thou art with me.

I need to keep seeing Jesus. Like Peter when he walked on the water, I must keep my eyes on Jesus so that I will not sink into the deep waters surrounding me (Matthew 14:22-36). Because I am human, the winds will frighten me. I will look away, begin to sink, and cry out: "Lord, save me!" He will reach out His hand and catch me, asking once more, "You of little faith, why did you doubt?" It seems Jesus wanted even more from Peter who had been the only disciple to take the risk. Rather, I think it is that Jesus wants more for us. He has so much for us if we keep walking in faith with our eyes on Him. Once more, I climb into the boat with Him, and the winds cease. Safe and secure, I praise Him. Thank you, Lord Jesus, that you expect more from me because of the way you love me and want more for me.

After crying through the music and allowing my thoughts and prayers to exhaust their interaction with the lyrics of Tammy's song, I began to write out my frustrations to my first therapist.

I was counting on you to help me. You hurt me, instead. Closure doesn't have to hurt so much, not this much, not this long. Why won't you help me? You said that "we are in this world to help each other through it." Help me ease the pain. Show me that you care. Help me say good-bye in a healthier way.

28

Come through for me. Come through this with me.
You were my first counselor. I let you in. Finish this
with me. My heart knows you as a friend. I had come
to hug you and say good-bye when I last saw you, but
we argued instead. Like the curtain that suddenly
swept its way across the room blocking my view of
my father's casket, your office door swung shut before me. I didn't get to say good-bye to you. We
recreated the whole mess, but this time, I was supposed to get to say good-bye. You wouldn't let me. I
wanted to tell you that I loved you and show you
with a hug that I am a good person capable of for-
giving, deserving of forgiveness for anything that you
may have against me, and also deserving of resolution. I had to show you the ugly stuff to receive your
help and heal.

She had told me that I didn't need her approval and that I
didn't need to say I was sorry to her. Once again, these responses to me confused me. She also told me that she was
counting on me to analyze. Doing so is one of my greatest
strengths and, paradoxically, one of my greatest weaknesses.
It became hard not to analyze, especially after there seemed
to be some secret answer in my relationship with her that I
would discover if I just analyzed everything enough. Talk
about making me crazy!

Why didn't I just go away, I asked myself. I tried. She was
everywhere on campus. I would go to the restroom or the
lunch area and see her. I would walk on a sidewalk and see
her or be on the other side of campus near the library,
waiting for a friend, and she was there. One day, my family
had been to a state south of us, and she was there driving on

the highway as well! I was always happy to see her, but it was so hard to break away again. I felt like I was riding on a pain-filled emotional roller coaster. I would try to stay loving and keep a sound mind, but the unresolved feelings with her and from my dad kept rushing back to me. In order to overcome those feelings, I dug deeper within myself to find more love in my heart for her. Then, I would make an appointment to try to work everything out. With this pattern, she was in my heart like family, like with my father, my love for her was deep, confusing and overwhelming. Losing her felt like experiencing the death of him all over again. The unresolved relationship with both was so excruciatingly painful. I analyzed incessantly, but could not resolve the pain. God forgive me for looking to others and leaning on my own understanding so much. Heavenly Father, heal me. Help me to forgive those who have hurt me. "For Thine is the kingdom, the glory, and the power forever. Amen."

The Experts Speak Out

In her book, *From Surviving to Thriving: Incest, Feminism, and Recovery* (1991), Dinsmore writes:

> Incest is traumatic. (Furthermore), incest robs children of their childhoods, of their sexual selves, of the basic ingredients for healthy relationships—intimacy, trust, boundaries, security, and self-esteem. . . . Regardless of its form and the child's response, incest is a devastating experience and leaves a devastating mark on its victim" (p.21).

> The recovery process takes place over time, and in-

cludes necessary stages that must be mastered; however, there is no one 'correct' process that must be followed. . . .There is no formula for healing. Women have facilitated their recovery process in many different ways. . . Incest recovery is a spiral process rather than a linear one" (p. 33).

The stages of incest recovery are acknowledgment, the crisis, the disclosure (to oneself and to others), depression, anger, mourning, acceptance and moving on" (p. 34).

The crisis after acknowledgment is a period of time when flooding of feelings likely occur and when things look much worse typically before they begin to look better. This is an "emergency state" where the therapist needs to be available in one form or another to the survivor 24 hours a day. This time of crisis is when the survivor seems to obsess about the abuse. Friends and family often do not understand and she/he feels abandoned. There may also be "flashbacks, nightmares, anxiety attacks, depression, suicidal ideation, withdrawal, and a loss of interest in other aspects of one's life" (p. 36).

To counteract this very scary stage where coping skills used as a child are being dismissed, a new exposure of the pain surfaces. It is at this time that many new and "life-enhancing" coping skills are needed, such as: therapy, art, music, exercise, prayer, massage, and reassurance. Self-disclosure is also vital in the healing process. The survivor needs to find wholeness within his- or herself. There is a need to find a place of belonging in the world with a sense of purpose and human dignity.

31

In His book, *Lasting Effects of Child Sexual Abuse,* (Wyatt & Powell, Eds., 1988) Roland Smith contributes that

> We have overlooked or outrageously trivialized this subject, not because it is peripheral to major social interest, but because it is so central that we have not dared to conceptualize its scope. Much as the individual victim is compelled into silence, self-punishment, dissociation, and identification with the aggressor, we as a society move thoughtlessly to deny sexual abuse and to conceal vast aggregates of pain and rage. Telltale outcroppings are resolutely covered over, fragmented, or mislabeled to protect our faith in a false concept of the status quo (p. 41).

I felt so incredibly abandoned by every human being in my life regarding the abuse. There was so much that I did not know or understand. I struggled to let people in or to express myself and often the words and the feelings would be lost in silence. The silence felt unbearably heavy at times.

In Carol Gilligan's 1993 publication of *In A Different Voice,* (1982, 1993), she writes about the silence as she contributes breakthrough research regarding girls' moral development based on caring. In Gilligan's work, she collaborates with her colleague, Annie Rogers, to:

> . . .speak of girls' losing their 'ordinary courage,' or finding that what had seemed ordinary—having a voice and being in relationship—had now become extraordinary, something to be experienced only in the safest and most private of relationships. This psychological seclusion of girls from the public world

at the time of adolescence sets the stage for a kind of privatization of women's experience and impedes the development of women's political voice and presence in the public world. The dissociation of girls' voices from girls' experiences in adolescence, so that girls are not saying what they know and eventually not knowing it as well, is a prefiguring of many women's sense of having the rug of experience pulled out from under them, or of coming to experience their feelings and thoughts not as real but as fabrication" (p. xxii).

Gilligan states that

Girls struggle against losing voice and against creating an inner division or split, so that large parts of themselves are kept out of relationship (p. xxiii). Bringing the experiences of women and girls to full light, although in one sense perfectly straightforward, becomes a radical endeavor. Staying in connection, then, with women and girls—in teaching, in research, in therapy, in friendship, in motherhood, in the course of daily living—is potentially revolutionary (xxiv).

To complicate this issue of silence, I was sexually abused during this time of adolescence that Gilligan writes about. This taboo experience in my life at age 14 was another force that silenced me. I recall having my own thoughts and hearing a significant voice telling me that something I said was "ridiculous." I am not blaming anyone, I am just sharing with the reader. With my first counselor, there were all these not yet explainable and expressible feelings, these taboo memories and dissociation or disconnection within myself, along with an overwhelming sense of abandonment for various reasons. I didn't know how to cope or what to do. I would try so hard to contain all that came flooding forth while also trying to deal with what was being contained and felt in order to heal.

Roger's book, *A Shining Affliction*, (1995) tells of Annie's experience of harm and healing in therapy. After a traumatic separation from her therapist (Melanie), Annie shares an insight that seemed too familiar to me. While at the office of her new therapist, "Blumenfeld," he quietly says to her

> Like your father, Melanie is really blind to you. She left you without ever recognizing you. That's not a goodbye, Annie; it's just leaving (p. 273).

During this time of her life, Annie was also doing an internship of counseling children. One child's name was Ben who touched Annie's life in a way that went beyond the realm of reality into a "magical" place where Annie's instincts and, it seems Ben's as well, were causing them to interact in ways that were deeply affecting the other's life. In reflecting on the closure with Ben, Annie writes:

> The loss of someone cherished and deeply loved is something every human being is confronted with sooner or later. But when an abandonment, a disastrous ending, imprints so much pain that life itself becomes a torment, as it had been for Ben, even as a baby, then the manner and meaning of leaving becomes vital. Such a leaving can be the shattering repetition of trauma, an ongoing nightmare from

which a child tries in vain to awaken. It can also be a healing experience even if saying goodbye is extraordinarily painful (p. 305).

With this goodbye that Annie was facing with Ben, she was also in touch with her loss of Melanie (someone who had once related with Annie with the possibility of adopting her, but later rejected this idea). As years of counseling continued, Melanie moved more into her therapeutic role while Annie was left to cope with these actions and her feelings about them. She writes:

> I think often about Melanie. My thoughts drift around a core of lasting sadness, sometimes tinged with bitterness, sometimes with compassion. My relationship with Melanie deeply affects my understanding of myself and my questions about clinical relationships, particularly among women. Carol Gilligan and I have often thought together about the particular difficulties women face in working in a traditional structure of psychotherapy—the desire by both patients and therapists for an authentic and enduring connection in a structure that upholds distance and teaches the necessity of giving up that desire (p. 312).

When I refer to my first counselor, I experienced my own "Melanie" relationship. I knew that many others were struggling and sharing painful experiences, but I had no idea how across the board this suffering occurred. Writing about the first therapist is in no way meant to point a finger at her, judge or persecute this woman. We were two people that God brought together for His purposes in a counseling arena

within the field of psychology. In my first counseling relationship, I learned a lot and have carried with me good
memories of our interactions as well as the painful ones—
even while I became further hurt. My family and friends' response to me when I tried to talk to them about this
situation was "let her go." I tried the best that I could, but
there she was—all over the campus, then all over the
campus of my heart.

In his book, *Adults Abused As Children*, Dale (1999) de-
votes an entire chapter of his text to "talking about abuse"
and the difficulty thereof. Regarding therapy, Dale writes
that

> not being able to talk is sometimes the major
> problem. Some clients initially get around this diffi-
> culty by developing non-verbal forms of communica-
> tion, including writing, painting, and sculpture. . . .In
> contrast to a total inability to talk about abuse,
> others are able to do this—but only in an emotion-
> ally disconnected way (p. 104).

In her book, *Learning To Trust Again*, Sands (1999) also
discusses this silence, referring to it as a "conspiracy of silence" in which "most victims are too ashamed to speak
out" (p. 19).

Spiritually, as well as in the therapeutic healing process,
there is power in the spoken word. Christ, Himself, is the
embodiment of the Word that is the Holy Bible, the good
news, the Word that was with God in the beginning and was
made flesh. To speak the Living Word empowers the person
in battle against spiritual darkness. This is true in speaking

about childhood sexual abuse as well. To have or insist upon the freedom to talk about childhood rape and to also speak and apply biblical truths and healing prayers empowers the one who has been harmed to successfully fight against the spiritual darkness and the accumulating negative effects of silence. Biblically, faith is key. Faith—being able to trust—is the remedy that is able to "move mountains." In a similar way, to be able to trust again, to speak out and be heard, and to be able to express and release the memories and the feelings that have been trapped within (while being accepted and embraced), moves mountains known as shame, pain, and other debilitating emotions. These emotions keep people stuck in their past and limit their ability to move freely in their God-given purpose. To feel rejected by the first counselor, while also pursuing further study in her field, was detrimental to my ability to heal, to move forward career-wise and to proceed with all that God had for me.

When a child has experienced sexual abuse and seeks to heal, there is not always someone there for the child to go to, feel safe with, or rely upon for help. After betrayal, it is hard to know whom to reach out to and whom to trust. To be further betrayed, abandoned, and rejected when risking opening up to someone who is thought to be able to help also damages the healthy need to trust. During these and later years, it is important that a trust in God is restored to be able to turn to Him for guidance, deliverance, healing, and comfort. Unfortunately, the restoration of trust and deeper spiritual intimacy in that very key relationship is often a process that takes many years. Some children hold this secret of sexual abuse years and even decades before they even feel that they can begin this process of healing. The shame and secrecy build havoc upon itself and too often do not allow for the incest survivor to receive another human being as someone to be trusted. The greater deprivation is the lack of or inability to receive a glimpse of God-like love and acceptance in this increasing and overwhelming void in their lives.

There is another struggle that takes place for the victim of childhood sexual abuse, and that is the difficulty of the Christian community to know how to handle the situation. So often Christians have an expectation of forgiveness without allowing time and the healing process to play its part in true forgiveness.

Vought (in Christa Sands book, *Learning to Trust Again,* 1999) writes,

> . . .when we pressure victims to let go of the anger quickly and forgive the perpetrator, we do not realize that premature forgiveness can actually hinder the healing process (p.9).

The pressure to forgive cuts off relationship and fellowship that is desperately needed and not received in the good intentioned bandage approach to what is an awkward and taboo crime upon the soul of a child. Sands describes this process as having to take "many issues . . .to . . .God's healing light" (p.13); a process that most often takes time.

Freedom is the goal, freedoms such as, freedom from the secrecy, freedom to trust again, freedom to be oneself, freedom to own oneself (including one's body again), freedom to speak and feel, freedom to live an authentic life in the presence of others, and freedom to receive the Word of God and the promises He has for the journey of those who have been sexually or otherwise abused in childhood.

Sands writes something extremely important that needs to be heard, especially in the United States today when so many people are fighting against the ability for certain freedoms of speech involving the Christian voice! She states

> Satan is out to demolish God's kingdom. What a better way than to harm children at such an influential age that the wounds they suffer can block them from experiencing God's love and healing growth for the rest of their lives? (p. 21).

She goes on to say that speaking out is a "powerful offensive weapon." As it says in Scripture, "Everyone who does evil hates the light, and will not come into the light for fear that his deeds will be exposed" (John 3:20 LAB). God "reveals the deep things of darkness and brings deep shadows into the light" (Job 12:22). Telling is so difficult, yet with the telling comes the truth that sets the wounded child of God free. Through the very act of communicating, we are able to find our lives more fully and freely as we abide in God through the sacrifice and resurrection of Jesus; the Word of God made flesh.

In her book, *In a Different Voice*, Gilligan writes,

> . . .(I) remember how it felt to speak when there was no resonance, how it was when I began to write, how it still is for many people, how it still is for me sometimes. To have a voice is to be human. To have something to say is to be a person. But speaking depends

on listening and being heard; it is an intensely relational act (p. xvi).

We are made in the image of God. Jesus, being the Word made flesh, is the Son of God. To have a voice is human and is of God. God's Word is the bottom line. His voice is victorious. In the course of our lives, we must listen to His voice and continue to speak out as He leads us. We must continue to face the voids and our own areas of abandonment of speech if we are to claim our victory and live in freedom.

Boundaries Revisited—Speaking Out

My dad often tricked me into a place of shame, loneliness and despair. I wanted my first therapist to be a friend to me, but she wasn't. To my first therapist I wrote:

> I want closure within the boundaries that give us both a sense of security; closure that merits honor, respect, and maturity. I want to be friends—not in friendship, but still friends. I pray that if you are strong enough to meet me in the goodbye that I am talking about, I am strong enough to meet you there as well, with God's help.

Good Enough

And I never did win the gold medal, but I gave it my best, my all. I did somersaults and cartwheels. I sang and danced and took a chance. Where was I running so fast? What was it that I could do for you? What did I think you could do for me? I wanted to be free.

Limitations, boundaries, twists, turns, and plenty of pain. Still, when all is said and done, anger remains. I want to fly . . . I want to fly. But I'm tired, you know, and giving is gone. And, I never did win the gold medal. Nor do I know the words to my song.

I struggled to understand the lessons forced upon me, but never understood. The timing of being pushed out of the therapeutic nest was incredibly awful. Our relationship had ended without closure, resolution, or a peaceful and loving goodbye. I felt dead inside as though I were David, in I Samuel 21, trying to escape from Saul and being refused life-sustaining bread. I felt like I was dying and that part of me wanted to die even more as I was receiving a cold and legalistic response to my pain and suffering. I struggled to embrace the pain and find comfort within myself even though I had yet to find the words.

Like A Child

Somewhere inside, something inside, like a child inside, I hurt. Somewhere inside, something inside, like a child inside, I want to be held. What hurts?! I ask. I don't know cries a small voice from within. I don't know. Does it matter it asks? Please hold me. I hurt! Let someone hold me. But what do I tell them? What hurts, I cry out? I hurt, I say! Like a child, I hurt. Please hold me.

CHAPTER 4

Lessons Too Painful
To Learn

Phone calls (part 3)

A problem began occurring prior to and after I left the college where I had the relationship with the first counselor. I kept getting hang up prank phone calls that seemed to happen after I had visited the campus. I called my first therapist and said, "When I'm in touch with (her) or on campus, I get a hang up phone call." Pause. "That's funny," she responded, "someone has been calling and hanging up on me too. We need not speak again." She hung up.

The following morning, I received yet another hang up call. I was devastated. If the calls I received weren't from her, why didn't she help me? If the calls weren't from her, could they be from someone that she confided in—a supervisor, co-worker, family member, friend? If the calls weren't from her, I had just dug myself deeper into some insane black hole in my relationship with her.

It was a crazy making time. I spent days literally bedridden. My body felt weak and would sometimes shake. Even when I called her to tell her about the prank calls, my teeth were chattering and my body felt so cold. My nerves were shot. What evil person was calling me and playing on my vulnerability?

In looking back, I think that there was something going on that God was just beginning to teach me about called spiritual warfare. Whether in regard to what I had faced in my childhood or with the additional trauma of therapy that often went against the grain of my Christian perspective, there seemed to be a force trying to keep me from overcoming. The spiritual warfare I had experienced felt very intense.

In retrospect, I feel as though God was beginning to prepare me for a purpose He had for me in His plan to set captives free. I believe that "the enemy," knew that I belonged to God and fought to stop me from my freedom in the Lord through whatever means he could. I believe in good and evil and that the "enemy comes to kill, steal and destroy" while Jesus came so that we could "have life more abundantly." The weight of the daily challenges, the additional sense of abandonment due to an upcoming move, the lack of resolution and sense of rejection with the first therapist, along with the spiritual and emotional battles had caused me to feel such heaviness that I became very pensive and tried unsuccessfully to lean on my own understanding. I became focused on those understandings that I learned in the field of psychology as well as through what had taken place with this woman who had become a central figure in my life. The weight of it all, along with other glimpses of things God revealed to me by others regarding spiritual warfare, became so oppressive that I became depressed. I would tell my children that I had to study (and I did some of the time reflecting in how well I did academically), but so often I just lay in bed depressed and suffering in pain and anguish at my overwhelming battles and sense of hopelessness. I did not know then how to access the spiritual tools that I needed to overcome.

I prayed and was involved in church. On a rare occasion, I read my Bible, not yet understanding the power of the Holy Spirit through it. I had the understanding that God was playing a part in my life. I knew that He had plans and a purpose for me, but in short, I felt beaten down and alone. I had no idea about claiming God's power and authority over my life and trusting God with the circumstances that I was facing or how to make anything better with the first therapist. I just knew that I wanted to get away from there and move to the familiarity of my hometown area. I didn't understand then how much the conflicts with counseling and psychology were spiritual ones.

That is when I mustered up all of the courage I could and went to her office and asked for a hug. I wanted to say goodbye peacefully and lovingly. Her door was shut in my face. I don't believe she had a clue about the gentle spirit of love in which I came to her to reconcile or the courage it took to face her. Part of the pain was that I didn't think it would have mattered even if she had known. The sense of it not mattering to her added disillusionment to me as she was in the helping field that I was preparing to join and it didn't feel like she cared in the least. All I knew was that my efforts to reconcile and have closure with her were met with her phone call to security, the type of action on her part that would serve to re-open the wounds for me. I left, but before her door closed, I placed my foot in the doorway and asked, "When am I going to get a prank phone call? Tonight? Tomorrow? When?" She told me that was "projection." However; I did receive a hang up call at about 8:30 AM the following morning. I thought it was her or someone she knew. I hope that I was wrong. I have never regretted the love that I feel for her or the move from that area. I have regretted and grieved the resolution with her that had been left undone.

The School

I passed by the school one quiet afternoon. The buildings were empty as they stood upon a hillside that I once climbed. The walls of brick were strong and tall, like the door that stood closed before me saying "You don't belong."

I used to cry out as I stood among the buildings, "I do belong! I do!" Now, I cry because I know I don't. The papers on my wall say Phi Theta Kappa and College Writing Award, 3rd place. Where did they come from?

Like the one that says Associate of Arts—what does it mean? What do I know? Except there is a dead end entranceway between the empty buildings and me, as well as a student parking lot and a visitor's parking lot. And even visitors must feel some sense of belonging before they park—don't you think?

So, do you ever wonder about heaven's welcome signs on a quiet afternoon? Isn't it nice to wish someone well and never have to answer their haunting calls on a quiet afternoon? Won't it be nice to drive along the beautiful countryside and never know the pain of the empty buildings upon the hillside or feel the tears on a quiet afternoon?

Tears, . . .I passed by the school one quiet afternoon. Do you ever wonder about heaven's welcome signs on a quiet afternoon.

I remember once trying to talk with the first therapist in what I knew was going to be our last session. I was so afraid that she would be confrontational with me and cause more confusion that I had a friend talk with me until it was time for the session. I felt so vulnerable and defenseless. I arrived finding her and several colleagues talking outside her doorway. I felt intimidated already.

When facing the therapist, I began slightly rocking back and forth in my chair at which point she told me that I had a deep underlying problem and needed to see a psychiatrist. I asked her why she said that. She replied "look at how you are rocking and staring at me." I told her that usually I don't even look at her (my eye contact decreased towards her along with my trust level). That day, I was fighting so hard to understand and make sense and resolve our relationship that I was afraid and courageous all at once. So, I was slightly moving back and forth as I watched her stand up and walk towards the window then turn to face me again with her accusation. . . .

Here, then, is my deep underlying problem: I hate sin! I hate our sinful natures! I hate that I turn on TV and learn about wars, child abuse, murders in the killing fields of Cambodia, in the Holocaust, and in our own streets and schools and families! I hate that little children go hungry and that there are people who are literally starving to death! I hate that people take it upon themselves to go against the things that God wants of us! I hate that people get into powers of authority and misuse them by saying things like "you have a deep underlying problem and need to see a psychiatrist." I hate when people frightened by their own human limitations hide behind therapeutic ethics to shut a door in someone's face, rejecting rather than loving another human being.

I hate sin! I hate that my dad sexually abused me. I hate that people do hate crimes. I hate that people often sue other people over everything and anything, and that there has to be so many walls of fear and distrust. I hate that people create riots for their cause as if riots are any more from God than the cause they are fighting for. I hate the loneliness of overwhelming insights as I look around me, insights that increase as God reveals Himself and His truth more and more to me so that I can see the evil. I hate that people don't want me to be so sensitive. How can I not be sensitive without shutting out the one Hope that has kept me alive?

We are all sinners. I am a sinner, but by the grace of God I am saved, yet I hate that which I am. I hate being a sinner. I hate sin. "The wages of sin are death," yet by God's grace alone I am saved. I am a sinner, yet I am His forgiven child; and, the closer I get to Him, the more painful it is to look around and cope with what I see. Also, the more I see, the more I have to seek forgiveness for my lack of faith and surrender these burdens to Him. I know that He will sustain me. He is the great Comforter! He is victorious!

I have grabbed onto what I've seen and looked at it with all of its strengths and weaknesses beneath the light of God's Word. I have looked at human blunder in comparison to the glimpses I have had of God's brilliance. The difference is certainly worth crying and rocking in our seats about as people go on doing whatever they want to do anyhow. In Romans 14:12-19, Paul responds to the words of the Lord in verse 11 which says that "every knee will bow. . .and every tongue will confess to God" by telling us that

> . . .each of us will give an account of himself to God. Therefore let us stop passing judgment on one another. Instead, make up your mind not to put a stumbling block or obstacle in your brother's way. . . . Let us therefore make every effort to do what leads to peace and to mutual edification (LAB).

The *American Heritage Dictionary* defines the word "edification" as "intellectual, moral, or spiritual improvement; enlightenment." When I look around and within myself and see the sin, I need not to judge or fear. Rather, I need to have faith that even with the murders and starvation I see, including the more subtle murders of the soul and starvation of love towards one another, that God is still in control. He is powerful enough to do the guiding. He knows the plan. The timing is His. He has the whole world in His hands. Romans chapter 12 talks about love. In verses 9-21, the scripture reads,

> *Love must be sincere. Hate what is evil; cling to what is good. Be devoted to one another in brotherly love. Honor one another above yourselves. Never be lacking in zeal, but keep your spiritual fervor, serving the Lord. . . .Bless those who persecute you; bless and not curse. Rejoice with those who rejoice; mourn with those who mourn. . . .Do not repay evil with evil. . . .As far as it depends on you, live in peace with everyone. Do not take revenge, my friends, but leave room for God's wrath. . . .Do not be overcome by evil, but overcome evil with good* (LAB).

I respond, "I know, Lord, but I've seen so much and sometimes I get so weary."

In Hebrews 6:10, Paul reminds me that "God is not unjust; He will not forget (my) work and the love I have shown Him as I have helped His people and continue to help them" (LAB). In Matthew 10:40 Jesus says, "Anyone who receives you receives me, and he who receives me receives the one who sent me. . . . Also (vs. 42), if anyone gives even a cup of cold water to one of these little ones because he is my disciple, I tell you the truth, he will certainly not lose his reward" (LAB).

As much as it depends on me, I just want to live in peace

with everyone. I hate sin, and I love people. I must have faith, no matter what happens, that God loves us all even more and has the whole world in His hands. Therein lies my "deep underlying problem" and the heart of One I always turn to.

In a Shining Affliction, Rogers writes the following professional insight that validates what I have observed, experienced and tried to communicate about the counseling field and counselor/client relationship:

> Interestingly, many of the therapists whom I talked to initially tried to break with the structured distance of traditional psychotherapy because it was not working. At first, their patients were relieved and grateful. But it seems that these therapist had no conceptual structure that enabled them to think critically about the changes they made, and no supervisory relationship that could support the intention of what was, perhaps, their most courageous work. Because this story is relatively common, I think that it represents a systemic problem in clinical practice.

> In practice; if we are uncomfortable, or truly frightened, we have a tendency to blame our patients and we have concepts readily at hand to effectively squelch any doubts about our assessment. Yet, in the act of defending ourselves, we are most likely to pass on our deepest wounding to our patients. . . .In any treatment situation, it is the therapist who is responsible for holding two stories, or two plays, together.

> We can be overwhelmed by these responsibilities.

We can then create a greater distance to protect ourselves, and even appear to be unmoved by our patients' responses to that distance. But the effect on our patients is deadening whenever we show them that they do not affect us (pp. 318-320).

Forever Friends

My hands are "empty." My heart revisits "broken." These are my friends. Tried and true—they stand the test of time. I can always count on them to be there. I call upon them in the special times. They always answer.

In the warmth of their company is where I find comfort. In the kindness of their midst is where I find mercy. In the flow of their tears is where I find peace. In the glory of their creator is where I find hope.

So, do not be sad or fret about nighttime's darkness. Look not to what is seen, but to that unseen song of celebration. Listen to that small still voice of the rising Son. For in the light of His grace is where I find salvation.

Tried and true, He stands the test of time; . . .and there, in the restoration of remembering, a quiet smile reaches my lips. Goodbye "Sir Empty." Farewell "Sir Broken." Until we meet again. . . . Until He comforts me again. . . .

Your Forever Friend

In August of 1993, I wrote the following words to my deceased father and the therapist.

It feels as though the two of you have ripped my heart out of me without mercy. The pain feels overwhelming, but I repeat the words of Terry Anderson to his captors of 2,455 days (They are a quotation from Genesis 50:20.): "You meant evil against me; but God meant it for good." May these words sustain me through the deliverance from my own private hell of captivity and torture, and may I always find hope and peace in the strength of God's victory and grace.

Boundaries

There are too many people with further psychological injury due to their therapeutic experience. It becomes so hard for them to trust reaching out again. In my own experience, I felt like I was walking a line between life and death so often only to stop just at the brink of wanting to die and crawl away to seek help. I somehow savored the morsels of "love" enough to choose life. I had lived for 20 years trying to cope with the haunting memories and the feelings that needed a safe place to be explored and expressed.

In all of the foolish games involved in the psychology of therapeutic settings, I had spent eight years actively struggling to get beyond the surface and focus of the therapeutic relationship and find the healing that I had been searching for. In all of that time, I had no true help to overcome the deep pain and anguish that I was feeling. I had found no human being yet able or willing to go the distance with me in processing and releasing the trauma that I was carrying within me. I was fighting with everything I had to survive the open wounds of the incest, while also striving to live my life successfully and sort out the semantics and limitations of the therapeutic setting and the counselors. I was crying out and begging to be able to get beyond the legalism and aloofness of the field and the fears of the unknown and have someone please get to the point and help me. I was literally relying on the crumbs I described earlier in "Curdled Love." If you read on, you will see more of my struggles as they become successes. You will see how I have chosen to fill the bottomless pit of being an incest survivor with a more focused personal relationship with God the Father, the Son and the Holy Spirit. In the midst of the oppression, there was at least one thing that went wrong for "the enemy." I began to notice that the more Satan messed with me and the more I suffered, the more I would turn to God and receive His gentle grace. I heard someone say once that this is because Satan does not have the fruits of the spirit such as self-control. He can't help himself. He persists until he drives a person right into the arms of Jesus!

Counselors have used this harsh and oppressive approach to try to coerce clients into the wanted changes that cause additional pain. Those who do so should question if their motives are purely to help others or out of a selfish need to appear successful, at least to themselves. They may ask God if what they are doing is coming from the enemy and not the One who has commanded us to love one another as ourselves. Changes out of fear and intimidation in counseling (and even in parenting or in any area where there is a person unequal in power structure), only serve to damage pieces of a person's soul and their ability to trust. This reflects directly in their ability to have faith in God. But God has won the battle and the victory is His. Those who are not for Him are against Him. So, those people in this debate about a harsh versus grace approach to treatment, ministry, parenting, etc., need to remember that we all have to stand before Him and be accountable as we face His judgment. We have to face Him when He asks if we have loved one another as ourselves. We need to take to heart Ezekiel 22:6-13. The Lord said,

> *See how each of the princes of Israel who are in you uses his power to shed blood. In you they have treated father and mother with contempt; in you they have oppressed the alien and mistreated the fatherless and the widow. You have despised my holy things and desecrated my Sabbaths. . . . . Have you forgotten me, declares the Lord. I WILL SURELY STRIKE MY HANDS TOGETHER AT THE UNJUST GAIN YOU HAVE MADE AND AT THE BLOOD YOU HAVE SHED IN YOUR MIDST* (LAB).

Biblically, we are to hate sin and not accept what people do against God and others. However, in secular psychology, we condone and even encourage sin with our acceptance of many behaviors that are against God (i.e., abortion, adultery, homosexuality). We do so in order to psychologically build the client's self-esteem and avoid the persecution of speaking the truth. We therefore, inadvertently, create in our world more opposition to the Word of God. We deny biblical truths just as Peter denied Christ as the latter made His way to the cross.

This is what the Sovereign Lord says, Strike your

*hands together and stamp your feet and cry out
"Alas!" because of all the wicked and detestable
practices of the house of Israel for they will fall by
the sword, famine and plague. . . . I will send my
wrath upon them. . . . They will know that I am
Lord* (Ezekiel 6: 11-14 LAB).

I strike my hands together, stamp my feet and cry out
within the pages of these writings. We are to discern but are
not to judge or throw stones, and we are to love one another—a delicate balance. Just like Ezekiel sitting on the
watchtower, I'm only accountable to say this once: Beware
of the father of lies through false teachers and false teachings such as can be learned through at least some areas of
the manmade study of psychology, particularly in the secular realm. Find the answers not simply in norms or statis-
tical experimental research, but in the Bible. What is the
norm anyway? The norm for me is God's chosen and called
out. The studies are fascinating and some findings are
helpful and from God, but what a leash I have had to keep
myself on throughout my studies and therapeutic experiences. It has been like tying a rope onto the tree of life so
that as I wandered through unknown areas, I could find my
way back to Jesus—the way, the truth and the life. He is the
only one that sets us free. I have claimed Hebrews 4:12-13
for the discernment of what is and what is not of Him.

*The word of God is living and active. Sharper than
any double-edged sword, it penetrates even to di-
viding soul and spirit, joints and marrow; it judges
the thoughts and attitudes of the heart. Nothing in
all creation is hidden from God's sight. Everything
is uncovered and laid bare before the eyes of Him to
whom we give account* (LAB).

The Bible says that I should not lean on my own understanding because God promises me that if I acknowledge Him in all things that He will make my paths straight. How many times, though, have I drug my brain into a state of confusion as I have strained my mind to find the answers and to figure it out without biblical truths to guide and empower me.

Psychology will keep me there in the secular land of the not there yet; like playing a game of solitaire—flipping cards and flipping more cards, manipulating numbers and wondering what would have happened if I had moved the other red nine or if only I had chosen that king instead of this king. I find the momentary joy of the win that lures me in again, but for what purpose? To relax my mind, to enhance my mind, to explore my mind, to entertain my mind," I try to convince myself; but, wait! I've played this game a 1,000 times. Alas, I win, and then, I get to play again. And what about that king I chose? What about that "King" I didn't—the One who has come to rest my weary soul? I hear Him say, "Beloved, beloved" (He calls more than once until I hear), "lean not unto your own understanding. . . . Be still, and know that I am God," and "I come to bring you peace," says the Prince. He tells me what I need to do; and how the secret is not a secret anymore if I simply "Love (Him) with all of my heart, and soul, and strength and mind. . ." because "He first loved (me)." So, come home little sheep. Come home to the land of "Yes, we are there!" We are where He is; where He was, and where He will always be. Come home to the promised land of milk and honey."

Seeing why He maps out commandments in stone, I ask once again, "How do I get there?" On the dead end avenues of my own understandings where the distance back remains the same, I am told to: "Love the Lord your God with all of your heart and soul and strength and mind" and believe and I will find Him there. No, not there in the self reliance called the game of solitaire—but, believe and I will find Him here where I find myself loving Him because He first loved me.

CHAPTER 5

Reaching Out for Help

With a cup of coffee in front of me, and a nice breeze circulating throughout my home, I read through some of what I have written to you. I took a deep breath and prayed,

God, help me to see clearly all that you have given me. Help me to receive great breaths of the life that I breathe through knowing you. Help me to acknowledge and receive the gifts that you have given me through the beauty of your creation. Heavenly Father, thank you for the sky, the birds, and the trees. Thank you for this beautiful day. Thank you for all of the wonderful friends that you have blessed me with forever throughout my life. Help me to step into the darkness that has haunted me; to acknowledge and receive all of the love, commitment, and dedication that my family and friends have given me; and to come out with your light shining through me. I can be so fearful of receiving the love in the ways that others are able to give. I can become so focused on the healing that I need from the sexual abuse and other obstacles to overcome in life, that I lose sight of the love and the light you have given me. I have a wonderful family and friends. God, you always send someone along who loves me. I am so thankful for their presence and support that it causes me to cry as I think of each person who has entered my life at various times throughout it. I stop and cry for "His eye is on the sparrow and I know He watches me." Thank you, Jesus.

For anyone who doesn't know this love from our heavenly Father and therefore doesn't have the greatest "resource" of all, please stop with me now and receive Him. Believe in Jesus. Ask Him to come into your heart and forgive you of all the ways that you (as I) have sinned. Let me hold you in this moment as He holds you, in whatever experience that you are having. Gently allow Him to dissolve the walls in your heart and fill you with the love and the power of the Holy Spirit. Give God your life. Let Him in. He won't hurt you. He loves you in a way that no one else can. If you need someone, reach out. Call on a friend or a pastor. Go to a church. Turn on the Christian TV station if you have it in your area. Read the Bible. Sing praises. Pray your own prayer. Let go and let God call you to feel whatever it is you feel. Respond in the way you feel called by God to respond. Find whatever it is you need and reach out. Reach out and never give up. "He healeth the broken in heart, and bindeth up their wounds" (Psalm 147:3). "Greater is He that is in

you than he that is in the world" (1 John 4:4). "When my father and my mother forsake me, then the Lord will take me
up" (Psalm 27:10).

> *Fear thou not; for I am with thee: be not dismayed;*
> *for I am thy God: I will strengthen thee; yea, I will*
> *help thee; yea, I will uphold thee with the right*
> *hand of my righteousness. Behold, all they that are*
> *incensed against thee shall be ashamed and con-*
> *founded. . .For I, the Lord thy God, will hold thy*
> *right hand, saying unto thee, Fear not; I will help*
> *thee* (Isaiah 41:10-11,13).

> *Do not be anxious about anything, but in every-*
> *thing, by prayer and petition, with thanksgiving,*
> *present your requests to God. And the peace of God,*
> *which transcends all understanding, will guard*
> *your heart and your mind in Christ Jesus*
> (Philippians 4:6-7 LAB).

For all of us who have been sexually abused and who
struggle with the betrayal and with the acceptance of our
own bodies, remember Psalm 139:14-16 (LAB).

> *I praise you because I am fearfully and wonderfully*
> *made; your works are wonderful. I know that full*
> *well. My frame was not hidden from you when I*
> *was made in the secret place. When I was woven*
> *together in the depths of the earth, your eyes saw*
> *my unformed body. All the days ordained for me*
> *were written in your book before one of them came*
> *to be.*

And God said, "Let us make man in our image,
after our likeness. . .so God created man in his own
image, in the image of God created he him; male
and female he created them" (Genesis 1:26-27 LAB).

Getting Out of the Bed
Inside of My Brain

Thinking back, I wanted to express all the feelings that were whirling around within me. I still needed someone whom I could talk to who could help me. I searched and I found a therapist who was not afraid to hold me in her arms. She promised that we would face everything together. Sometimes the pain and working things through felt impossible; but consistently—even though sometimes sporadically, she kept her promise to be there with me. Commitment, like the importance God places on covenant throughout the Bible, are of high value in any healing process.

I wrote hundreds of pages to my new therapist of what I was feeling and thinking. I wrote freely, without censoring what came from me, and she read it all. I mailed her the letters or dropped them by her office via her mail slot. I also used crayons and colored pictures of the scenes I kept seeing regarding the abuse. When the time for closure came, I was angry. This process had become so much a part of my life. Also, I re-experienced the deep pain of my relationship with the first therapist. We struggled through even this. I needed to accept her wherever she was in our relationship and say good-bye. For the time being, I needed to feel the loss and move on.

When Willows Weep

Blood. Bond or Bondage? I don't know.
    Weeping willows.
    Winter, summer, spring or fall
    They've always wept.

Echoes of past resound themselves into the present.
    Reminders of being shut out,
    pain spirals abruptly back
    through the echoing rings.

To the center of the heart. My heart aches.
    A hand—mine—touches
    my heart
    and works to embrace. . .

Ah! Ow! As if the pain was physical. God?
    Tears. . . .Jesus wept.
    Dramatic? Would rather not
    have to be. Pain.

My life. . .The best that it gets. . .I am in love. . .
    with my successes.
    Triggers, transference,
    countertransference.

On ground level, woman to woman meet.
    Eye to eye,
    heart to heart,
    no more objectivity.

Active, reactive, disruptive. Distance. Time.
    Slipping in and out

as convenience calls
or hearts will.

Shame. Why didn't I hug her when she hurt?
    Why isn't she
    hugging me now?

It's the game of the open hand as I yank mine
    from my heart
    and reach it out
    before her.

Memories. . .of her hand reaching back and holding mine.
    A child playing
    beneath the branches
    of her luxurious new home.

Grass, soft and cool
    beneath bare feet,
    housing large strong
    roots.

Roots, reaching out seeking nutrients. . .love.
    Bond or bondage?
    I don't know.

Weeping Willows.
    Winter, summer, spring or fall—
    they always weep.

CHAPTER 6

Deliverance
in the Midst of Chaos

A couple of years after I ended my counseling relationship with this therapist, I received a phone call to participate in a survivor's group for childhood sexual abuse. I decided to join and see where I was with everything. I thought I could work a little more on closure issues and could possibly be helpful within the group. I felt that I still needed to heal some from my relationship with the first counselor because I felt drawn to the field of psychology and was working in social services. Further healing seemed like it would directly benefit my career. I was interested in possibly going to graduate school, pursuing my original goal of working out my own sexual abuse issues and then helping others. After joining the group, I received six weeks of individual counseling regarding the unresolved counselor issues. I learned that my first therapist did what she felt she could within the parameters of our relationship. I learned that my words are not only heard, but that I need to be cautious about their impact. I learned that I need to be open with people who know how to care in the ways that I need and that it is okay to need others and ask for help. What I needed to know even more deeply and intimately is that God's strength is made perfect through my weakness, that He loves me with an everlasting love, and that He will never leave me or forsake me even as I have felt others have.

At that time, I went to a poetry reading being held at the crisis center. There I learned that one of the counselors who facilitated a survivor's group I participated in a few years earlier had died and so I wrote the following:

Arriving at the poetry reading in that building they call the safe place, I'd almost given up looking for you there. It has been some three years since I have seen your brown eyes with straight brown hair combed toward them. Remember when I called you up and hugged you over the phone? Step by step, you asked me to describe the hug—the hug the way that she had taught me. You were like that, you know, questioning with your small step approach and your "not unlike" comparisons. I always knew I could count on you to get me to the places in my heart that I didn't know how to take you to.

Here we are together now in the building they call

the safe place. I have come for the poetry readings on rape. Unknown to me was the reading of your words, your poem. "You had died," the Director said. I didn't know. Then came the scheduled rape poems. They moved me, but were not so moving as you (as is the power of those who make it the safe place). I kept my composure until I was out in the parkway where I heard an injured wild animal crying out into the darkness through my own mouth. The sobbing sounds begged for you to still be near enough to hear that your life had meaning to me. I hoped out loud that you were blessed to see the earthly lives that you had touched in "passing." It was a priceless gift you gave: yourself to others; to me. Thank you for your poem. You are with me even here in the safe place I call my car. You have given me comfort. We shall also celebrate, for you are well now. Your worries and pains are gone. Rest peacefully, my friend.

"Foolish Games" Phone Calls (Part Four)

A few days after I learned of this counselor's death, I received a phone call from a detective regarding letters I had written to the first therapist. Why would she do such a thing when all I had sought and reached out for was a peaceful ending?

Sharing about the situation with the incest survivors group resulted in a meeting with the two therapists and their supervisor to discuss a fourth therapist (the one whose detective had called). I received a recommendation that I see a fifth therapist. This all seemed crazy. While waiting for the meeting, I felt warmth, more like a sensation of heat across my heart and arms. I spent the time praying and receiving the warmth sensing that God was healing my heart. I invited the warmth to linger as I thanked God for the healing touch, love, and total sense of His presence that I was experiencing. I asked Him to be with me in the meeting. I did not talk of this to the therapists, thinking that they would not recognize God's hand in my healing, and not wanting them to distract me from the power of His presence upon me.

I am experiencing the same sensation as I express what happened. The warmth is lingering and I just want to cry as I feel God's loving presence once again. And I do. Release me from this bondage, Father. Take from me any remaining bondage. Take away any remaining anger and fill me with your Holy Spirit. The warmth is still with me. I receive You Father. I receive You, Jesus. I love you. I thank you and praise you. I made it through the meeting as gracefully as possible, opted to see no more therapists and that night I wrote:

Dancing With My Father

Being "politically correct" holds no candle to "analytically critical." My brain thinks in the realm of the latter, a form that inspires therapeutically brilliant landscapes of joy minus those surfacing splashes of bright red blood—the blood of my self-mutilated heart. No scissors needed, no razor, no cutting tool other than the analytically critical gift bestowed upon me by the Father, distorted by my dad, and re-inforced by those of my choosing, and those less under my control.

I am the victim of therapeutic brilliance. "Does it help?" I ask in my standard form as the therapeutic high of witnessing the transformation wears into pain and sorrow—my withdrawal from the high. But God is near. Jesus sings to me through the words of R.E.M. "Everybody hurts sometimes. Everybody cries." Tearfully, I smile at the image of the hillside dance I have with Jesus, the man with the crowds that I turn toward to "take comfort in a friend." With my head resting gently on His knee, I cry "Oh Jesus!"

The term "enmeshment" therapeutically creeps through my mind. The genius over all mankind smiles at my analytically critical approach. We dance on the water. Eye to eye, I hold His hand. We laugh. We smile. We play. We dance in pure joy. "Immerse me. Enmesh me," I pray, as that which is therapeutically brilliant holds no candle to the experientially bright light of seeing beyond the faith and fear of walking on water. Down from my therapeutic high, we dance on the water. Down from my self-induced drug of choice, I am centered in the brilliance of His plan. Never a hallucination; but, grounded on the water, our spirits soar.

In retrospect, I wish I had never written to the first counselor. I wanted so much for her to be a part of the resolution I had found. Instead, I felt incredibly oppressed by her actions.

Several weeks later as I was asking God for help regarding my feelings, a comforting feeling came over me along with the thought to write to a former college professor who knows both the first therapist and me. I told him about the six weeks of therapy that allowed me to accept my accountability more fully, as well as provide me with more understanding and insight as to where the first therapist may have been coming from. I explained the detective's phone call that came just as I was at peace with the closure, the phone calls that I was falsely accused of making, and the Christian approach I used.

I explained that my heart was really bleeding. I described my struggle to find peace within myself again. I said how I regretted the mistakes I had made, and how no one likes to think of their alumni with such a sense of discomfort and pain or in a very realistically unsafe place. I questioned how, since so many years ago, she somehow has had the power to make the campus feel unsafe even in my heart as I succeeded very well there and had established positive relationships with all the other staff and faculty members that I had met. I also described the positive interactions I had simultaneously experienced when I represented the agency that I had worked for at the campus where I had earned my undergraduate degree. I felt falsely cast so negatively by her, treated so harshly, and cut off so severely. I asked for comfort and insight from my past professor as someone who knew me in a positive light and who had seen my academic success. He responded thoughtfully and with care. In God's mercy and grace, a man of God, this Christian friend, was placed in a haunting and hurtful situation, and he chose to allow God's compassion to shine through. In this way, I could receive insights that were helpful.

Closure seemed to be about letting go of the burden of responsibility in areas where I wasn't the responsible one. I needed to let go and give the responsibility for things to the One who is really in control—God. I feel that it has only been through love, respect, trust, and the presence of God in my life that I have been able to make progress in therapeutic relationships complete with human error and additional suffering. I wrote:

Lord, I need you to come through for me. I cannot do this life without you. I need you, heavenly Father, to take these burdens from me. I need to leave them on the laps of those they belong to. I need to sit with you on your lap. Oh God! I need to "come unto you" as I have been "burdened and heavy laden," and you have promised to give me rest. Despite all of the obstacles, all of the opposition in this topsy-turvy world and the "helping" field of psychology, and all of my mistakes, I have remained committed to you. In the end, despite the suffering I have experienced, the most important thing is that I have worked very hard to be obedient to your word. I have "loved my enemies" (Matthew 5:44). I have sought the truth and the teachings of the Holy Spirit—the Almighty Counselor. And, as Jesus said in John 14:31, "the world must learn that I love the Father and [being that I am an imperfect person, I strive to] do exactly what my Father has commanded me to do—love one another" (see John 15: 9-17). Forgive me, God, when fear and pain harden my heart. Thank you, Jesus, for bringing me through the storms. Thank you, Father, for all of the blessings you have given to me, your child. In Jesus' name, I pray. Amen.

Dear Therapist,
You may be discrete; but still I know your strengths and your weaknesses. I know your heart (or at least I know the pain, frustration, confusion and fascination that draw me to you again and again). Your nurturing and wisdom become the bottle of botulism that I swallow thirstily and naively. How would you know that in all your objectivity and arm's length ethics that in my desire to be one of you, my heart and eyes open themselves to you? Not able to grasp a full description, I always know something of your limitations, your defenses, your persona, and your spirit. So focused, yet never seeing the one item of most importance—the way both of us manage to make my heart ache. My heart aches for the insecurities that are beyond our freedom to speak about in this man-made therapeutic world. Still, in knowing the heart of you—my aching heart deepens, my need for love increases, and I pray: "Dear Jesus, fill that depth with your presence, your love, your healing; my Counselor, my Father, my Friend." As I pray for His guidance, His purpose, and His plan, a revelation comes to me. I am to love you. So; I write this letter generically "Dear Therapist," yet to each of you I write with all of my love. . .to a therapist, from a friend.

My prayer became a request for God to take away my focus from the therapists in my life. I asked Him to fill my heart with love for them and even forgiveness in the case of the first therapist. I asked Him to put my focus on Him instead as my healer. I prayed, "Heavenly Father, show me more of you. Let me feel you in my heart again. Help me in my un-belief."

He Called Me

In the early morning hours, He kept calling me. Did He still love me? Did He forgive me? Finally, I went to the stereo system and listened to the tune that kept playing in my head. It was a Righteous Brothers' song that spoke of the power of God being able to turn the tides and calm the season. It talked about how sad He is at how we live, but that He will always forgive. I sobbed as I heard the Righteous Brothers sing this song over and over again.

I remembered singing these words as a teenager in a church duet with a close friend. I cried out to God "How did I get so off track?" Through my chosen field of psychology and through counseling I learned so much. Yet, when I followed my Christian teachings of loving one another as God first loved us, I kept getting hurt and even rejected by one therapist. "Oh Lord," I prayed, "help me rise above those things that have taken so much of my focus. Show me your love. And, thank you for the weight that you've taken from me. Thank you for choosing me and bringing me through the evil destructiveness in this world and in my life. Thank you for the special love that you so deeply and intimately have shared with me through these hours in the early morning. The birds sing so cheerfully and the CD plays so divinely and interactively as I hug my Bible close to my heart and cry for hours while you sing to me. Praise you most merciful and gracious Father. Amen."

Praise God because just around the time of the detective's call, something wonderful happened regarding the second therapist. Before I tell you what that is, let me fill in some details. The second therapist is the one that I described earlier. She was unable to help me with the incest, but I originally had chosen to see her because she was the counselor at my undergraduate college. I felt that I needed to face my fear of being on a campus again following the rejection and pain I experienced from my first counselor. I pray for God's blessings upon this woman whose greatest help was the way she always welcomed me back even after I had graduated.

Within a week or so of the detective's phone call, I had to set up a display on campus for the social service agency I worked for. The representatives from the various agencies setting up displays were provided a lunch. The second therapist came in and I watched, ready to greet her as she looked towards the table of food. When she saw me, I reached out my hand towards her, and she came and held it as we talked. Then, she sat by the campus head security guard while we all ate. Before I left the room, both of them were refreshingly friendly and professional. They both welcomed me to come back again anytime. Can you imagine how healing that was in response to the first therapist, her security guards and the phone call by the detective? A miracle from God occurred in His perfect timing so that I would be able to have contact with this woman. I felt the grace that could have only come from the all-knowing, omnipresent Creator! Since that day, I've seen this lovely person on a number of occasions. She has always welcomed me and introduced me to others as having been a student at that campus. What a blessing she became to me!

After I said goodbye to everyone from the childhood sexual abuse survivor's group and while preparing to move to another state, I realized that it had been years since I had contact with one of my counselors. I contacted her, shared with her that I was moving, and we decided to meet for lunch.

Since then, our relationship has consisted of lunches together when I am in the area, e-mails and occasional phone conversations. We share thoughts, feelings, our professional experiences, our personal lives and love.

We are open with one another and with this area of our relationship as friends—even while remnants of therapeutic boundaries remain. We look at this new territory of our lives together as well as learn from the counseling relationship that we once had. Because the territory is new, we take our time with it and rely on our hearts and safe boundaries to pave the way. I once wrote the following message to her regarding our friendship:

> It was one thing when you and I were working together, and we would help me make huge amounts of progress. Then came all of that separation, individuation and boundary focus that still leaves me feeling insecure in our relationship. It is a source of weakness that leaves me always to wonder when you are going to tell me suddenly that our friendship isn't one that I can count on—not in the sense of being free to come and go as we need, but in the sense of a cutting it off completely. A final separation would bring me to a place where I am left to try to go on with my life even while that brokenness in my heart is always a part of me to struggle with and try to reconcile from time to time—no matter how far I have come, a place that leaves me to wonder about my inadequacies in relationships and in life.

I wish that I had the confidence and social skills that I had before all of the psychology. I wish that all of my moves combined with all of my counseling experiences would have made my insecurities decrease instead of increase. I wish that I had known how to turn more fully to God earlier on to fill the gaps sooner and not leave myself so open (not vulnerable which I am being here with you now) but open to those things that are hurtful more than they have been helpful. Love is very powerful though. I don't regret the love in any relationship. . . . Love is the greatest thing. I don't regret it even in the cutting off.

God's love is so great that no matter what, nothing can separate us from it except our choice to refuse it—that act being spiritual suicide. That choice to be cut off from Him must be so painful to Him like that choice to be cut off from one another is so painful to us. In death, there is always the pain of loss, but the hope of a future together in heaven with Jesus.
In suicide, there always seems this final angry statement of revenge even though there is much personal pain, confusion and depression. There is this cutting off that leaves people with a lifetime of so much pain to resolve as best as they can and to hope that it is not played out in other relationships. Abortion is about that cutting off—demonstrating that the woman doesn't want the child even though the child was placed in her life. I think therapy is to help those who are cut out of a relationship just as in abortion or suicide.

Maybe there are other places we could go together or things that we can do or ways that time could be spent, but there is no place between us more important than the place where our hearts meet. That is love. Love has nothing to do with individuation, uniqueness, diversity, relationship with others or even the roles that we play. The role is simply the vehicle that allows the love to happen in whatever way it is needed. A role is just a vehicle—a movable, flexible mode of transportation. The vehicle transports love and healing. Sometimes, the vehicle serves the best purpose that it possibly can and the role changes—not flippantly or haphazardly, not in a perversion of the love, but in allowing the flow of it to continue with healthy love, whole love, agape love. From that place, I never regret the love. I only regret when it is not received because then I do not feel free to be at home inside of myself, inside of my own heart to express the love that is there. I hope to continue to move with you in the direction that the love is flowing. Hold onto the love. Hold onto the fresh breath of life that each new day brings. You have my heart and my thoughts in response to yours. I love you.

I am thankful for my relationship with this counselor who has become and remains a faithful friend. At the same time, I felt that for my personal and professional progress I still needed to heal in relationship to counselors in general. I chose to see a counselor to help me with a counseling class assignment given during graduate school. The assignment included choosing a real issue. It was difficult to lean on the counselor at all. I did the assignment and came to a good place with the work that we were doing, thanked her and was on my way. The following paragraphs are part of a letter that I had given to her:

In reaching out to you, I feel like I can let go of the chip on my shoulder regarding counselors and move forward in my work even though I know that God is the Only One that I can fully rely on. I do love you. I love all of the counselors I have met no matter what—even if I have been told that I am not supposed to. Most of all, though, I love the Counselor of counselors. I love God. (His strength is made perfect through my weakness.)

I have felt really oppressed in counseling relationships at times. Writing has become my outlet. Always, I believe that God's dreams are better for me even than mine are for myself. So, I keep holding onto my faith and keeping my focus. There seems to be a door opening for publishing. I have been so programmed to be silent and go away that it is an effort to walk through that door, but I vow to keep walking in faith. I don't know how things will unfold, but I know that God will shine His light on each step of the way and that He is always with me—even when I am afraid. Thank you for having been one of those who He has sent to help me.

As for reaching out, I'm thankful for many friends, teachers, role models and mentors that I have been blessed with along the way. There are those in my life who have remained devoted and present. There are those who made room and allowed me to talk about my deepest secrets and heartaches while crying in their arms. There are the ones who overcame and who succeeded in various ways in their own lives, who knew how not to stay stuck and somehow took me with them through and beyond the areas of being personally immobile. Ultimate freedom is found in God and in His love for us, but we still need one another. These are my friends. These are my teachers of life.

Inside the Circle

could I cry from your words
their gentleness
the touch of them upon my heart
words, like flesh, tangible, touchable
ssssh, their sweetness. . .so still. . .
within the center, within the circle
within this holy place, within inside
where love embraces
your massage of tender places
now safe with love that never fails
and never shall

I go away when love whispers
I will never let you
I will never let you
chase away or run
beyond the freedom of ourselves together
your whispered words, your gentle touch
my heart cries tears of joy
inside our circle
our love holds me

CHAPTER 7

Believe in What
You Believe In

As I read back through my own journey, there is one thing that does make sense to me and that is the command to love one another. One of my pastors years ago spoke the following words in one of his sermons: "Believe in what you believe in." Somehow those words provide me with some sense of grounding. Throughout my spiritual and psychological journey (having been a psychology major, there is a definite connection and a definite difference), I must return to the cross and to the life of Christ for guidance.

There may have been moments in these pages where I have discussed salvation as if I have some holy hold or authority on the subject, but God knows as you do having read these pages that I mess up like everyone else. I have revealed myself, but struggle that some of the things I say are somehow offensive. I worry about all that is so human and not Christlike in me. I find myself ashamed sometimes for being descriptive of the incest; yet knowing that the shame doesn't belong to me and is in place only to hold me captive. There were moments when I had wished so desperately that I would have had a safe place to go, parents who were faithful to one another to consistently protect, soothe and care for me.

One day several years ago, I cried and cried until I got up from my sofa and drifted over to the tapestry of the Last Supper that hung on the wall of my family room. I reached out and held Christ as I leaned against the wall feeling the softness of the fabric. I remember the woman who came into the alley near where I lived as a child while I was playing. She showed up from somewhere to ask, "Do you know God?" I had grown up in a Protestant church during my ten years of life, but I really had to think about her question. What was she talking about? What did she mean? Why was she asking? The woman stayed in contact with my friends and me. She helped us with our plans to put on our carnival for Muscular Dystrophy.

That summer my friends' mom had cancer and was dying. I went to a revival at their church and watched my friends go to the altar during the call to receive Christ into their lives. I thought of the altar call and of the woman in the alley. "Did I know God?" I wanted to receive Him into my heart. My friends' mom went to heaven that summer. I accepted Christ and also received eternal life. Do I know God? Sometimes I see Him in my life so clearly. I try so hard to surrender to His ways and His plan in my life choices. Sometimes the path isn't clear because my own will blinds me. Sometimes listening is so hard to do. Sometimes life hurts so much it confuses me. In Tammy Trent's song, "Run to the Cross," she tells us to run to the cross when we feel like we can't go on because Jesus is waiting there ready to bear our pain. Running to the cross and believing in what I believe in, I need to tell you about:

Green Beans & Ice Cream

Let me tell you something about my dad. There were actually good memories with him that I want to hold onto because they are mine every bit as much as the difficult ones I have focused on. The best memory is this: my dad supported my ideas. When I suggested planting a garden to help our family eat more economically, my dad gave me the money for seeds and his blessings in digging up the yard. Once started, my dad came outside and helped me dig. Then, we went to the Dairy Queen.

When I had a wild idea about taking our station wagons to the mountains for picnicking, fishing, and sleeping over, my dad listened to my plans and we went. It is a cherished memory even though no one could sleep, my mother had fears of mountain wild cats of some kind, and we eventually had to drive home. That is the day I caught a hook full of crabs, left my fishing pole behind and excitedly ran to where my parents were together preparing our dinner. Later when we drove down the mountainside in complete darkness, I saw my first deer in the middle of the road.

Let me also tell you about the time my dad was playing

music with his band in the hall they had rented. My dad came down onto the dance floor just to dance with me at the age of seven. I felt so special—like the queen of the world. The musicians would come to my house and music would sound throughout and we would have lots of great food and lots of laughter (my dad often made people laugh). We would also go to their homes for the same good times. This fun was something that my dad brought into my life.

I think that my dad was proud of me in a way. He always encouraged me to sing at these various gatherings. My dad brought the music into my life that allowed me to enjoy traveling with Christian music groups and making an album. That was my dad's gift to me for joy in my life. My dad reinforced my laughter with his, my sense of humor with his, my love for music with his, and my work ethics with his. My dad supported my ideas and accomplishments so that I could go on to succeed despite his criticism and abuse.

Dad, we did have a relationship that mattered to me. I did love you. I do remember you carrying me through Grandpap's yard to look at the beautiful flowers he had planted. I do remember all of the laughter and silliness we had at mealtimes. I do remember those evenings you were so happy to bring home special goodies for us to eat, giving us celebrations. Dad, I do remember how you hugged my mother in the kitchen, and sang with her to the music you played on your guitar and how good that made me feel. I do remember how hard you worked to provide for us. I do remember how much you struggled, how much you couldn't sleep at night, and how much your body hurt. Daddy, I do remember you seeking help from your oldest sister, my aunt who has now since passed away. Dad, I do remember that you had time to play the guitar with me. I do remember that you made time to come see me in various dance and school activities. Dad, I do remember you trying to make me be the best that I could be. I do remember your interest in the planning of my wedding. I do remember the loan you took out for it, as broke as we were. Dad, I even remember the pain that you shared when someone had done some injustice to us or when my nephew, your grandson died that week before you. And, Dad, do you remember my no bake cookies and the routine in which I cracked my knuckles? I can hear your laugh. Did you know that I loved you? I hope that you were wise enough to see beyond that wall that you forced me to build around myself to see that I did.

Dad, I deeply loved you, always. You see, that is why you were able to hurt me so much. And now, your picture standing alongside my mom watching me in my wedding gown (with me holding my Bible and flowers) remains in the ceramic heart-shaped frame Mom bought me. I still love you despite the pain you have brought to me. Dad, I am the conductor of my orchestra. This is my command performance for you. I still love you. We are still growing our garden: Green beans, ice cream, and love.

Joy. . .imagine that

In my life, I struggle over all the things that people struggle with who have not been sexually abused and broken in childhood. It is very important for me to keep balance in my life with family, friends, church, writing, and work. I need to play. I need to laugh and have fun. I need to be childlike and silly. I need to touch, and kiss, and hug the people I love. I need activities like amusement parks, skiing, volleyball, picnics, and walks in the park. I need to kiss my kids and spend time with them in ways that I hope I've done enough of for them to remember. I need the memories of my trips to California, Mexico, Niagara Falls, Toronto, and Florida. I need the memories of those airplane rides, "The Phantom of the Opera," and the ocean. I need music, and fresh air, and the entertainment of my daughters' sports (written in the 90's). God has blessed me in so many ways. I have been loved. I have felt joy. . .imagine that. . . . Thank you, dear heavenly Father.

Reflections

As human beings, we need to create order in our lives. As communicators, we need to create words that express meaning and feelings in order to build relationships. As psychologists, we need to experiment and use words and statistics to categorize and understand human behavior. So, for example, when someone is sexually abused, we call that person a victim. We say, "the victim responded this way or the victim felt that way." When someone is victimized, they may be prone to further victimization by having lowered self-esteem and a poor sense of personal boundaries; however, the word "victim" in itself may place limitations on the person.

It seems to me that once the sexual abuse is completed, the person is no longer a victim, but a survivor. Once the survivor finds the courage to place his or her hand on the telephone or reaches out for help to someone in some way, then there is hope and even the word "survivor" becomes limiting. In every small step, in every expressed thought or feeling, there is hope. If in fear the person pulls away or falls into "old familiar, self defeating" patterns of behaving, the seeds have still been planted and there is hope. When we are available to touch one another, there is hope. When we are capable of saying the words, "beyond sexual abuse," there is hope. As God fills the empty places inside of me, I feel less and less resentment for labels and categorization. As I grow and am better able to love and respect myself, I feel my uniqueness. As I continue to accept all of myself, I continue to heal and feel less controlled by the sometimes limiting words we use as human beings, communicators, and psychologists.

In the previous pages, I have rarely, if at all, referred to statistics. I am not about facts and figures. This writing is about connecting in love, and it's about hope. I am thankful for all of the courageous women who have shared their incest stories. These women who have shined their lights on a subject that society has wanted to keep in the dark, have given me strength, hope, and an easier journey. Still, we need to learn the steps of our own dance to be free.

At one time I was a contact person for a local Survivor's group. My name was printed in a directory and I received calls from people long after the group dissolved. Many of these calls were from women. I made referrals and spent a little bit of time on the phone listening and sharing, assuring them that they are not alone. Many of the calls came from men, as well. My heart has gone out to men because they are, as one therapist has said, "the last taboo." I care very deeply about these men and am pleased that more awareness and opportunities for healing are becoming available to them. I'm not sure what the differences are, if any, between men and women in their efforts to heal. Supposedly, women tend to turn their anger inward, having more of a tendency to self-abuse or attempt to commit suicide, whereas men supposedly tend to cope with trauma and abuse by being abusive to others (perpetrating). I am not making any generalizations across the board at all; such generalizations would only serve to keep "the last taboo" alive. I do know of a man who not only discusses his childhood sexual abuse, but his having grown up to be a sexual abuser. He talks courageously and openly determined never to hurt anyone again. I cannot know a lot about what it is like to be this person. I just pray for the healing of his heart.

There was another man who once called me. He seemed young and still under "the spell" of a perpetrator. While he didn't live at home, he would still visit there where he would go into a dissociative state and the hypnotic-like suggestion and follow the words of his stepfather. I empathetically told the young man to simply stand up when this happens. He had been crying, and it was if something clicked for him. That is all he needed to do. Stand up in a very literal way, and stand up for himself as a child of God. It seems so hard to imagine that anyone could hold this kind of trance-like power over another, yet somehow shocking and terrorizing situations do often cause us to freeze, especially if we feel helpless or lost in the inability to cope. Our bodies respond this way to physical trauma. They may numb out in areas or we may even go into a coma or have amnesia. I think that God has made us this way to help us survive somehow.

Someone once told me that what we do to survive as children will often destroy us as adults. I just wonder in what areas I still need to learn to simply stand up in, giving the power and the glory to God and feeling really good about myself for being His. The thing is, I believe we all have areas that have a hold on us like the man who called me—smoking, drinking, overeating, adultery, anorexia, bulimia, etc.; his just sounds more unbelievable because it is so devastating. I pray for him even at this moment as I did when he and I hung up that night of the phone call.

> Dear God, you know who I am talking about. Please give him the strength to simply stand up and the opportunity to experience the goodness within himself as a child that you love with all of your heart. Thank you, heavenly Father, for allowing me the honor to be helpful to him through the conversation that he and I had. Thank you for always being there for me to pray to, for the words to say and for the ears to really listen when I know that I, in myself, am too weak to give what he needs—that which only you can fulfill. In Jesus' name, I pray. Thank you, Lord. Amen.

As for the women that I have encountered—those who are therapists and survivors, as well as those who come together for any purpose, I have written:

Women

Together, a delicate strength, we walk a fine line as
    friends—not always in friendship.
We share our hearts (if we dare) and listen, listen,

shh—be still and listen to the others.
Learning to trust, to sense—to feel, to see, to hear
    whatever forms can be spoken.
Separately, a common bond threads through us the
    experiences of our past.
And, as women in our world,
    beautiful designs of differences weave throughout
    the likeness of our beings.
We, the takers of risk, the deliverers of life,
    seek to create adventures as great and wondrous
    as they can be,
While seeking simply to be loved as we are
individually women.

Stones

One of my therapists likes stones. As I was preparing to leave my house (on the afternoon when I had cried listening to the CD and asking God to help me rise above those things that have taken so much of my focus), I heard Neil Diamond sing "she would ache for love and get but stones." I wondered why stones were so important to the counselor. She told me that if she turned every stone, doing so in itself would make a difference in the world. I wondered about the song's meaning.

I thought of the lepers being outcast by people who feared the disease that ate away at their bodies. I thought I had read about stones being cast to keep the lepers at a distance. I remembered the stone that I received for reading a poem in a group. The stone says "survivor." For a while, I kept the stone on my dresser along with another one I found at a loved one's graveside. I thought of the lepers being like incest survivors and of the isolation of both experiences. I remembered Jesus healing the man with leprosy (Mark 1:40-42 LAB). The man came to Jesus and faithfully risked begging on his knees "If you are willing, you can make me clean. Filled with compassion, Jesus reached out His hand and touched him" and he was cured. When I am feeling isolated, outcast, and beyond the understanding of others, I can trust that Jesus is willing to be with me and, see, touch, clean and heal me. He does not go away or send me away from Him. That is the best part. Humans are like wildflowers at best who grow on stones and find sunshine in the warmth of one another's love. But God is always with us. When our hearts "ache for love" He brings us "the Christ, the Son of the Living God" (Matthew 16:15-18 LAB). Our God heals the sick, touches the outcast, calms the seas and gives us peace even during those moments when we, like the lepers, ache for love and get but stones.

Jerusalem's Stone

I think of the women who had returned to the tomb cut in rock (Luke 23 and 24) where Jesus' body was laid. Bringing spices to the tomb, they found that the stone that had blocked the entrance had been rolled away. Today people travel to Jerusalem to see the tomb. The stone is still rolled away and people can see the empty tomb, a "wasted" tourist attraction in the sense that there is nothing there. It is just as the angels asked, "Why do you look for the living among the dead? He is not here; He has risen!"

I believe in the stone that had been rolled away—Jerusalem's stone—like the stones that block our hearts from everlasting life. I believe that He lives and I ask Him to "light every star that makes my darkness bright and to keep watch all through each long and lonely night." I will continue to remember the women who have served to counsel me. I will always love each one in the beauty of her strengths and weaknesses; but most important, the Lord has released me and sets me free in Him. He has shown me the way. Thank you, God, for being at the center of yet another new beginning. Continue to remove the stones that block my heart and prevent me from letting your love in. Thank you for your unfailing love. In Jesus' name I pray. Amen.

Bringing Light

Throughout my writing and my counseling and educational goals, I wanted to bring light into an area of darkness and to serve others as Jesus asks of us in Matthew 25:34-40. Verse 40 says, "Whatever you did for the one of the least of these brothers of mine, you did for me" (LAB). I say that because through my experiences, I know what it is like to be emotionally starving, thirsty, a stranger, unclothed, sick and imprisoned. We all do at times. And, we all long for those on His right (verse 34) to not only feed and clothe us literally, but also to give us drink, to invite us in, and to visit us when we are sick and held captive within our hearts. I have longed for other's obedience in the darkest times and places of my life, as I have also longed to bring the same Christian love to others.

As I read and feel my way through the pages that I have written, I find that I am there for myself in a way that no one else could possibly be by turning to Jesus in those bleakest of moments. The more I have focused on giving through the efforts of these writings, the more I have re-

ceived for myself. The only way I have ever found to bring
light into the darkness has been through God. To para-
phrase John 3:16; God sent Jesus into the world because He
loves us and we need to be saved from ourselves and the evil
that keeps us separate from Abba, our heavenly Father
God. He sent Jesus, the resurrected Christ, to show us the
way. He gave us His only Son, the Way, the Truth, and the
Life so that we may have eternal life. In His giving, God
wants each and every one of us to be His people, as He
wants to be our one and only God. He wants a relationship
with us. He sent His perfect Son to suffer at our hands, die,
and arise from the dead to forgive and free us from our
sinful nature. We simply need to surrender our wills and let
them die in obedience to God's will for our lives. If we let
Him, if we love Him, if we let Him love us, if we trust Him,
we can be reborn, free and forgiven from our sins. For the
choosing, He immerses us in His love, in His forgiveness,
and in His mercy. "Praise God from whom all blessings
flow!" Praise God for wanting our attention, our obedience,
our love, and no other gods before Him.

Along the way, I have become focused on so many false
gods—food, money, psychology, others' love and approval,
and the sins of others against me, including incest. Let me
tell you that again because if you are a survivor of incest
and in the depths of your pain and anguish and longing for
healing, this admission may be difficult. As Christians, we
need to realize that we haven't kept our focus on God when
the evil of incest creeps upon us over and over again, like
"slithering Satan snake fingers." There is a haven to rest in.
There is the grace of God. There is freedom. "Jesus Christ,
superstar, do you think you're who they say you are?" Yes!
You are. Forgive me, Father, for I have sinned.

Lord, a while ago, I stopped praying that you would change the therapists into what I needed them to be, but rather that you would take my focus away from them. And, You did. I had tried, but could never change my focus onto You without Your help. As I discover that I have made the subject of incest and the pain and sense of isolation a god before You, I need You to change me. I need You, Lord of my life. I need You, the one and only most awesome God. Thank You for Your unfailing love. Help me to let it in, to forgive, and to feel Your forgiveness. When I mess up (which I will), help me to start anew with You. Give me the balance that only You can give.

God loves you, too. Jesus once said, "Come ye who are burdened and heavy laden and I will give you rest." I have been asked to "love the Lord, my God, with all of my heart, with all of my soul, with all of my strength, and with all of my mind; and to love my neighbor as myself" (Luke 10:27 LAB). On the very first page of this writing, I gave only one condition to you for turning the pages that you have in your hands. I asked that you do what God has commanded for us. I asked you to love one another. Apparently, you have read the pages for you to be here with me so far. Have you loved one another? Have you loved the Lord, our God, with all of your heart, soul, strength, and mind? I know that I have a lot of work yet in areas in which He seeks to change me if I let go of my will and let Him. Go to Him with the areas of your life, no matter what they are, wherever you need His help for you to do His will. Go to Him also if you are burdened and heavy laden. He will give you rest. Read Hebrews 13:1-5. He will never leave us or forsake us. So often I forget: His love is perfect. His love is unfailing. God never fails. No matter how anything appears, as long as I abide in Him and walk in alignment with His plans for me, I have not failed either.

Sometimes people learn to trust God and focus on Him for a while to know that God's Word does not return void. In Psalm 121, our Creator of heaven and earth promises not to let our feet slip as we rest in the comforting knowledge that He is watching over us. In Psalm 73, Asaph confesses his own sense of failure as he loses his focus on God's goodness. He speaks of his flesh failing, but enters into the sanctuary of God and embraces our heavenly Father as his strength and his refuge. God breaks the strongholds and becomes our "good stronghold in times of trouble" (Nahum 1:7). See Psalm 73 where we enter into the sanctuary of God, where He is with us to counsel and to guide us and afterwards He takes us into His glory—then on and on from glory to glory. Part of the beauty of Psalm 73 is that Asaph was humble and honest enough to actualize the failure paradox. The admission to God that Asaph had lost his focus and felt like he was losing his testimony and foothold was exactly the admission that actualized his faith. God is good and would not let Asaph fail. All that Asaph had to do was turn to our heavenly Father, entering God's sanctuary with praises and thanksgiving for God's goodness to prevail.

It is in God's greatness and goodness and in His worthiness that we come humbly before Him proclaiming our smallness, unworthiness, and inability to succeed without Him. It is in His goodness, mercy and love for us that in the midst of our failures and sense of unworthiness that we enter into His sanctuary, where we see that He is worthy, where we experience His glory, where it clicks somewhere within us that

He longs for us to be His sons and His daughters and experience the richness of His Kingdom that is and is to come. Here we can find our confidence in Him and hold our heads up as His children. It is in His sanctuary that we see beyond our failures and the traps of the enemy to keep us from fully lifting our heads, our hearts, our hands and our voices to the heavens. Look up. See His face. Receive His grace. Believe in the truth of His word. Walk in His light. In Him, you are worthy; so take that one small step of faith and "Believe in what you believe in." In Jesus name, I pray. Amen.

CHAPTER 8

A New Beginning

. . .forgetting what lies behind, I press on toward the goal to win the prize for which God has called me heavenward in Christ Jesus (Philippians 3:13).

Dear heavenly Father, I ask for Your help that I may focus on what You have for me. I pray that the joy of You continuously outshines the darkness of these pages. As I open my heart to You, I also ask that what men/women knowingly or unknowingly intended for evil that You use for good, and that together, we create a new beginning, one that is fresh and anew in joy and praise for Your kingdom that is and is to come. In Jesus' blessed and holy name I pray. Amen.

ear Survivor, You are my friend at a level and language
that no one can understand without having been
taken where we have been. I have come to a place
where others' inability to understand is acceptable because,
out of love for them, I wouldn't want them to have to understand. I know how much the abuse hurts. Even though it is
time for me to seek God for healing and turn to others for
love and prayer, if you called me in pain and anguish, I
would likely refer you to a therapist just like I would refer
someone with a broken arm to a doctor.

Still, there are two roads in life to choose from. If you need
to seek help from a counselor, seek God first then reach out
for wise and godly counsel. Psalm 1:1-3,6 says it this way:

> *Blessed is the man who does not walk in the
> counsel of the wicked or stand in the way of sinners
> or sit in the seat of mockers. But his delight is in the
> law of the Lord, and on His law he meditates day
> and night. He is like a tree planted by streams of
> water, which yields its fruit in season and whose
> leaf does not wither. Whatever he does prospers. For
> the Lord watches over the way of the righteous, but
> the way of the wicked will perish* (LAB).

I have seen a lot of evil in my life, but nothing compares to
the pain of sexual abuse, particularly incest at the hands of
a parent. I hope you can feel my love because it is at this
level and beyond that I believe Jesus knows, understands,
cries with you and feels compassion. A relationship with a
therapist is a very special one. A relationship with the Holy
Spirit is even greater. Ask God to help you feel safe in Him.
Ask Him to protect you from yourself; especially if you are

self-injurious in anyway. Let God be your release. Let Him catch you when you fall into the darkness of pain-filled memories. Surrender to Him everything that hurts. Ask Jesus to help you experience His resurrection in your life. Ask God for courage, comfort, and strength. Ask Him to ease your pain and focus you on His will for your life. I know what it takes living in the excruciating pain of sexual abuse, and I know the additional pain and the trust required to go under and allow the surgeon's knife to take the cancerous tumor from your soul. Hold on, walk, run, dance, crawl, or rest peacefully in His arms. I love you, but His love alone is unfailing. "The Lord longs to be gracious to you; He rises to show you compassion. For the Lord is a God of justice. Blessed are all who wait for him" (Isaiah 30: 18 LAB).

Pressing Into Love With Him

I have looked for help in so many directions only to return to God's love every time. I want to deliver His love to you like the best of fine foods on a silver platter. I want to, but I can only praise Him for being all of the things to me that I cannot be for myself.

> Lord, I seek Your truths and Your guidance because You never fail me. Sometimes, heavenly Father, I look at the situations around me and make decisions whether they are good or bad. I may think of the incest or my dad's death, or my having to move out of state and question You: "God do You hate me?" But somehow I listen for Your answer and I hear You say that You love me. How do I explain anymore clearly how we can love ourselves simply because we are Yours? How do I say to look for the light of God's

love in everything? How do I show how much I love You? Your love sets me free. Your love is greater than anything I have written about in these pages. I look to You for my answers. I run to You with my pain. I lay it before You, the resurrected Christ, the living God, my heavenly Father. You take it all because that is Your purpose. Your job description is all encompassing of my every need. Your timing is perfect when I align myself with Your plan for me. When I wait upon You, Lord, You renew my strength and mount me up with wings as eagles. I fly so high! Look Mom, no hands! And, the funny thing is that I may be in flight and not even know it. I may be saying "No. Lord, I can't do that." But then I surrender and before I know it, I am feeling the freedom of my open heart, wings extended fully, the soft breeze against my face, and the joy of knowing-knowing absolutely, without a doubt that You have me and You love me for I am Yours and You are mine. I praise You, oh God, with laughter and singing and writing and dancing. Free this child within me, Father. You are mine. And, You are all that others need, as well. How do I tell them?

I will try to tell about the gentle power of God through a story: When I was a case manager for a Christian foster care agency, a little boy came into my life and quickly worked his way right into my heart. During one of our last moments together, he left me with a statement about the power of God.

This little boy and his mom were extremely close. His love for her was so intense that he fought during visitations to stay with her, and we needed two case managers to take him back to his foster home. Once after he spit at us, screamed for his mom, and continually struggled to get out of his seat-belt, he finally became totally exhausted. I looked through my rearview mirror to see him asleep in my coworker's arms as tears of love and empathy were streaming down her face. I did not stay with that agency very long, but along with what my supervisor gave me to complete before leaving, I asked God, "Lord, what do you want to accomplish through me before I leave this job." He gave me about ten things. How do I know that they were from God? I know because I couldn't have pulled those things off on my own will. The main task was to reunite this little boy with his mother.

On the drive home from the court hearing, this time the four-year-old boy joyfully sat in the back seat. This time, he was there with his mom and he asked her to read the up-coming road sign. She said that she couldn't see it because she didn't have her glasses on. He yelled out with all of the trust and innocent conviction that only a child can have, "Are you blind, Mom? Cause if you're blind, you just talk to God because He is a powerful man, and He will help you." What insight and wisdom from a little boy. My friend, can you see? "You just talk to God because He is a powerful man, and He will help you." Give Him all of your heart. He already knows it, so tell Him everything you need to say. Talk and/or write to Him. He doesn't need to have you censure anything. Be united or reunited with Him.

There is evil in the world and free will. We have eaten from the tree described in Genesis, so we hurt others and others have hurt us. God sent His Son to save us. Give Him your heart—all of it. Look to Him for what you need. Stay in the midst of others who have found Him. Read the Bible and other writings that you feel He is speaking through to you. Listen for God and see Him through the mouths and eyes of little children—even when the honesty of their words may not feel so good. God bless the children. As children of God, "just talk to Him because God is a powerful man and He will help you." Even if you feel unworthy, tell Him. Even if you are angry with Him, tell Him. Even when you doubt His existence, tell Him. Even when you think he hates or has forsaken you, tell Him. Ask Him to show you His love for you. Ask Him to help you in your unbelief. Ask Him to show you the way to rise above and fly as the eagles do. Then when He does, because He will if you only faithfully let Him, give praise to Him for He alone is victorious. He alone can make the difference in your heart. I've searched, but there is only one answer—one answer in three—the Father, the Son, and the Holy Spirit.

We need to take whatever pain and burdens we are carrying to God. Just let them go. He is truly merciful. His love is triumphant. I am nobody apart from Him. And no one can ever separate me from His love. He and I are bonded beyond the horrible trauma of incest. I will fight every emotional battle, every deception from Satan, every evil thing done against me to keep the walls of pain from blocking my heart and vision from the always and forever presence of God, our Father, Abba. The best part of this fight is that the battle belongs to God. To Him be the glory!

Lollipops and Love

God always provides for us. Just as He freed the Israelites

and promised them the land bountiful with milk and honey, we need to keep our focus on God instead of on our fears. In our fears, we look at the Promised Land only to see the overwhelming size of the devouring giants. (Read the Old Testament book, Numbers, to verify what I am saying.) Having been held captive and hurt in the past, we become afraid to trust. We transfer that lack of trust onto God, but God always provides.

There was a time when many people in my life had talked with me about cancer and other physical problems that seemed to be taking the lives of their loved ones. Even in my work, I talked with people who were crying about the loss of a loved one. Listening to others at that time, I began feeling my own grief regarding my dad as well as empathy for what they were going through. My grief began to feel overwhelming, so God gave me scripture to trust Him. The reminder that God had brought me through other things renewed my faith that He would bring me through this emotional pain. It had been difficult, but I have remembered to keep my eyes on God in the midst of my grief.

There was another foster child that I had worked with—another little boy who was not permitted to have visitation with his mother for a short time. When he came to my office, I offered him a lollipop because it was all I could think to do for him. He talked about his mom, so I asked him if he would like to write his mom a letter that I would hold until we could give it to her. He was only six-years-old, but communicated his heart beautifully. Basically, he wrote that no matter what she had done to him, he still loved her. Enclosed with the letter was his very favorite flavored lollipop that was to have been for him. Can you believe the love in his heart?

One night, I awoke to my own grief. Like I had often done, I sat alone on my bathroom floor crying and praying. I didn't want to awaken anyone. I didn't want anyone to see me that way. As I prayed for Jesus to hold me, my husband came into the bathroom. There were times when my husband was unable to be there for me emotionally, but God was making changes in him. That night, I let my husband into the private places in my heart (changes in me, as well) where he held me as I cried and talked to him. In the midst of what has seemed like bad times when many marriages break up over fears and financial stress, our marriage grew stronger than ever. He held me in his arms until I was done crying. He told me to always wake him up so that he can be with me when I'm hurting like that. Then, he asked me if I would like a drink of water. The cup he used reads: "Someone loves you . . .me." It was so sweet how he pointed out the words on the cup that he used to bring me water.

God used my husband to show me that I am loved not only by the man I have been married to for over 27 years, but by Jesus, the Living Water. I just have to open my eyes and see. I just have to open my heart and receive. With God's help, I made it through my grief. And you see, I do wish with all of my heart that I could give my favorite lollipop to my dad. Still, there is a loving man right here that deserves my favorite lollipop. And there is my heavenly Father who deserves my favorite lollipop. Thank you, Jesus, for allowing me to witness the love in a little boy's heart, for letting me receive the love in a gentle man's heart, and for Your love.

Euphoria, Humanism, and Healing
The revival in my soul lasted approximately 12 spirit-filled

hours, or so I thought at first glance. The morning following my lollipops and love writing, I had not had much sleep. Still, I felt joyful and energetic as I shared in praise and worship with my church family. After the service, my sense of euphoria came crashing down as I was looking inside an entertainment center at church to see if by chance (certainly not by clear communication) some videotapes that I needed to coordinate a class were waiting there for me. Wrong! The shelves were empty, which was fine, except that a woman followed me into the room and announced from out of nowhere "There is nothing in there. . .the book shelf is empty." Those words "nothing in there" and "empty" hit me like lead weights. In a daze, I followed the woman out of the room in which I suddenly felt I had no right to exist in. My walk took me into her office where she started looking on a shelf for something. I found myself dazed and staring at a turkey that appeared to be wooden with tail feathers made of all different colors of lollipops. I do not know what was said between the woman and myself. I needed to tell my husband what had just happened.

Soon after my conversation with him, something clicked about the turkey in the woman's office. Earlier that morning, I had prayed that God would find a way to put a lollipop in my life to symbolize our special relationship and His love for me. In the midst of my joyful spirit, I had forgotten the prayer. In the midst of my discouragement, I stared at the turkey with its lollipops, not connecting why I was so drawn to them. You see, God drew me into the room at the perfect time to show me how special our relationship is—not just in my euphoria, but also in the midst of discouragement. A spiritual high feels wonderful, but healing comes God's way—even as spirit-filled down times when there seems to be nothing but emptiness.

God loves and forgives me just like the little foster boy had done in his letter to his mom. God gave me a rainbow of His favorite flavored lollipops as tail feathers on a Thanksgiving turkey. He made them all and reminded me that He loves and forgives me no matter what. I am thankful.

Ask God to remind you of His presence in all times. Keep your eyes open for His answer. Wait for His perfect timing. Praise Him for the gifts He gives. Abide in Him. For Jesus said in John 8: 31-32: "If you hold to my teaching, you are my disciples. Then you will know the truth and the truth will set you free" (LAB). I wanted the truth to lead me to a healing of continuous spiritual euphoria so that I could witness to you God's healing. In 2 Kings 5:11, God healed Naaman of leprosy; however, this healing did not occur the way Naaman thought it would. So, Naaman was angry and said, "I thought that (Elisha) would surely come out to me and stand and call on the name of the Lord his God, wave his hand over the spot and cure me of my leprosy" (LAB). Then, "He turned and went off in a rage." After some feedback from Naaman's servants, Naaman obeyed the original directions to receive healing. "He went down and dipped himself in the Jordan seven times, as the man of God had told him, and his flesh was restored and became clean like that of a young boy."

Naaman was a proud man used to getting great respect because he was a great hero. The Jordan was small, dirty and humbling. In humble obedience, Naaman received God's healing touch upon him. In my life, God has healed those areas of my "leprosy" (which I've written to you about earlier on); but like Naaman, I have had to humbly wash myself in the dirty waters that were not of my choosing. I wanted a miracle in which God would simply wave His hand over the spot and cure me. I have often turned from Him in rage thinking what a witness it would be if God would just do so, but God has other ways of fulfilling His will and using me to fulfill His purpose. I share my healing through moments of pain, rage, and becoming humbled in the filth of the dirty water—water that the provider of living water uses to heal me. While this is not my picture of healing and health, I know it is of God. Perhaps His way has been for me to write my witness to you—to share His truth with you. Some people will tell you that there is no such thing as truth—that there is my truth, your truth, and some truth that may or may not have anything to do with what either of us claims to be true. In Jesus, there is all truth and "the truth will set us free." To God be the glory! Amen.

Reunions

God's healing hand reaches through hardened hearts
    when hearts cry help
And hands' fists unclench
    little by little by little
To trust a touch
    as a longing heart wills a reunion
        octaves beneath tears' pond.

Pondering at ground level (the question drowned no longer),
    the quivering voice asks, "God, will you hurt me too?"
God's loving eyes
    turn to joyful tears as He knows the reunion is at hand.
His hand reaches through a hardened heart that now
    knowing the truth forgets the question.
Hungering, needing, receiving, happily hanging in there
    holding on to the touch

Opening wide heart's arms
The wings of eagles in flight fly exuberantly
   into the embrace that existed all along
      within the palm of
God's healing hand.

God said "Press onward. Listen to my words. Hear my words. See my words. Hold them in you hands—in your palms. Let go of that which is of the world. Hold onto my words. Hold onto me because I am your heavenly Father who will never leave you nor forsake you."

Dear heavenly Father, I hear You and surrender to Your Word that I may claim the power and the victory that is beyond all evil; for You are the Alpha and the Omega, the beginning and the end. Your love is everlasting. Your knowledge exceeds all brilliance. Remove and cast away the power of my dad's words on me. Cut his words about my hands from my heart, my mind, my soul, and the memories I have held. Remove the symbolism of abusive behavior that he gave me when he rubbed the palm of my hand. I couldn't make it go away. The counselors couldn't remove it, but You are able with just one touch of Your healing hand.

Dear Jesus, replace in me the power and the joy of your resurrection and life everlasting. Oh Jesus, let me feel in my palm the cross that I hold up high for all to see. You have not left me. You have only left the tree—the tree that held You to its arms by nail holes meant to "kill, steal and destroy," but You arose to set me free from my sins and the sins of others. To God be the glory in the name of Jesus, through the blood of the risen Savior, Christ the Almighty, whose name I have been given and claim to cast out the evil while Satan smiles in defense—his only recourse for he has lost the battle and tries to deceive me into thinking otherwise. God has shown me what lies beneath the smirk that condemns the serpent to an eternity of defeat. God has given me Himself. I offer my thanksgiving through an embracing of His gift.

My Goliath

When I first went to college, my goal was to face myself, examine and heal my own wounds, and help others. Sitting on a hillside with a friend and looking out across the skies and the land, I remember searching for what I was experiencing and telling my friend that I felt like I was a part of something really big. I told her that I didn't know what that something is, that I may never know, but that I could feel myself being a part of whatever it is.

Along the way there have been great joys and sorrows. Around some turns in the road I have had to face my Goliath. For so long, I took on such responsibility for the defeat of him, taking what seemed a lifetime to learn that the battle belonged to God. Like David, I was to remove the armor that was too big (the size only emphasizing my smallness and fear) and only served to add weight to my life and an additional burden to bear. I am to use my stone and slingshot, aiming with deadly accuracy, but it is the Lord who delivers me from my Goliath and removes disgrace from my life. The battle is His, not mine. The outcome is for His purposes, not mine. I set a goal to work through my "stuff" so that I could help others. My plan was to become a counselor. I picked up my stone and slingshot and aimed with deadly accuracy at Goliath; but in fear and smallness, I still wore the armor. God has been helping me to remove the weight as I practice my walk trusting Him without it.

I still think I am a part of something so much greater than me that I may never know what it is—except that it is of God. I do not know whether God will ever want me to become a counselor. Maybe it is more like the movie "Mr. Holland's Opus," and maybe this book, or simply my process in writing it, is my opus. I don't really know how or if God will use it. I only know that He led me to keep pouring my heart out on paper. I only know that God can renew my strength if I wait upon Him. Only in Him do I mount up with wings as eagles. Only in Him do I run and not become weary. Only in Him do I walk and not faint. (See Isaiah 40:31.) Only in Him do my flying dreams come to life. I am alive in Him. I have new life through my relationship with Him. Whatever my purpose is, God knows the plans He has for me. He is the conductor of my orchestra.

The Love Relationship

The Bible describes what love is throughout its pages. Love is not in food, alcohol, drugs, cigarettes, philosophy, or psychology, at least not the kind of love that is long standing and doesn't let us down. Love that stands firm is in God alone. As for other religions, I have learned about them enough to let them go from within my mind because there is no love so filling to me as the love relationship with the one and only God: the Father, the Son, and the Holy Spirit. There is no other religion that stresses the importance of relationship as Christianity does. Only God has all the answers and we are to come to Him as children (Matthew 10:25). God wants us to seek Him persistently. Matthew 7:7-

8 reveals to us that if we "ask, it will be given; seek, and we will find; knock, and the door shall be open" (LAB). He has wanted a relationship with us since the day that He created us (read Genesis).

> *Love is patient, love is kind. It does not envy, it does not boast, it is not proud. It is not rude, it is not self-seeking, it is not easily angered, it keeps no record of wrongs. Love does not delight in evil but rejoices with the truth. It always protects, always trusts, always hopes, always perseveres. Love never fails* (I Corinthians 13:4-8 LAB).

There is something in this love relationship so substantial that other religions are pale by comparison. The love relationship with God is a personal one.

In Exodus, Moses talked with God as a friend. In John 15:15, Jesus called His followers His friends. In the Garden of Eden following the consumption of the forbidden fruit, God walked through the garden asking Adam, "Where are you?" Of course, He already knew because God created us and knows every hair on our heads, but Adam had to speak out in the midst of his shame. He had to confess that he had hidden due to his nakedness and fear. As we often do, Adam blamed someone else—Eve, who quickly blamed the serpent's deceptiveness. God brought discipline to all three as sin separates us from Him. Through grace and the risen Savior, we are forgiven. Love is John 3:16.

With regard to psychology, I felt disconnected and dehumanized by various approaches throughout the years. I felt discord being associated with Jungian thought, object-relations, or any other secular model that approaches the effects and treatment of trauma and fits people into boxes. What a contrast to share my views from a Christian perspective that provides me with a greater sense of wholeness! I have traveled many roads where I have been lost and so off track in my search, that the only association I want to be identified with is my relationship with God through the love offering of His only Son. Jesus resides within us (if we receive Him) through the power of His Holy Spirit.

Jungian or any other analysis may provide insights, but they hold no candle to the answers found through Jesus Christ our Lord and Savior. "Seek and ye shall find. . .knock and the door shall be open." His is the love relationship that frees us from our captors. We only think we are in control or that some religion of the mind can save us. We search in all the wrong places resisting our need to repent and submit our wills in obedience to God. We hold onto our worldly wisdom, concerns and control as if they are something that will save us. What if in the midst of holding on tightly, we hear God gently say, "Let them go. . .just let go"? The truth is that God already has full control. After all, He is the Creator of heaven and earth. He just wants to hold you in His arms, comfort you, and give you rest. This is the Love Relationship that makes all the difference.

Several years ago, I went to visit a friend who gave me an important message that in retrospect encapsulates much of what I've been trying to share through the experiences of my life. She wanted me to hear a song by Bob Hartman on a "Never Say Die" CD by the Christian music group, Petra. Some of the lyrics describe a woman named Annie who lived alone in her desperation and committed suicide . The song goes on to share how although it was too late for Annie, it's not too late to share with others that Jesus loves them. My friend died exactly five years prior to this section of my writings. What she knew for herself and would want me to tell you, I express here for both of us in honor of her life. Jesus loves you! He truly cares. He can free you. He bears your burdens and your pain. "It's not too late."

Open Doors

A professor and friend once said that we should never say "no" to ourselves when we come to reaching out for something that we want to achieve. She said that there are enough people who will say "no" to us and to our dreams, so we should never close the door on our own selves.

I think of her wisdom as I think of our receiving the grace of God's forgiveness and our eternal life with Him. I have to admit that there are some times when I feel so small and become afraid—and I need to keep those words in the forefront of my thoughts so that my own fear does not cause me to say "no" and close the doors on myself. God is still working with me on some things, but I am so glad that I have said "yes" about stepping out in faith to receive eternal life and trying, through His help, to abide with God in my walk.

In a beautifully dramatic style, Max Lucado captures in his book, *On The Anvil,* what this "open door" to God looks like as he connects the days of old with these "last days." Mr. Lucado writes:

The annual event always drew a crowd. The priest would

solemnly ascend the temple steps, cradling in his arms a lamb. As the people waited outside, he would pass through the great curtain and enter the Holy of Holies. He would kill the lamb upon the altar and pray that the blood would appease God. The sins would be rolled back. And the people would sigh with relief. A great curtain hung as a reminder of the distance between God and man. It was like a deep chasm that no one could breach. Man on his island . . .quarantined because of sin.

God could have left it like that. He could have left the people isolated. He could have washed his hands of the whole mess. He could have turned back, tossed in the towel, and started over on another planet. He could have, you know. But, he didn't.

God himself breached the chasm. In the darkness of an eclipsed sun, he and a lamb stood in the Holy of Holies. He laid the Lamb on the altar. Not the lamb of a priest or a Jew or a shepherd, but the Lamb of God. The angels hushed as the blood of the Sufficient Sacrifice began to fall on the golden altar. Where had dripped the blood of lambs, now dripped the blood of life.

"Behold the Lamb of God."

And then it happened. God turned and looked one last time at the curtain.

"No more." And it was torn. . . from top to bottom. Ripped in two.

"No more! No more lambs! No more curtain! No more sacrifices! No more separation! And the sun came out."

112

God, through the shed blood of His Son, has ripped the curtain in two. He used a curtain. He didn't use a door that He closes again and again. He has grown us deeper in His love and in our relationship with Him and forgives us of our sins. There is no more separation despite us! We must learn through faith not to hang our own door. Through faith, we must remove the padlocks and proceed to let Jesus in to take our lives and mold them into the best that they can be.

It is just as the professor, also a believer, had spoken: "We must not close the door on ourselves." Open the door and see. The curtain has been ripped, "And the sun came out." And the Son has risen as we look at the empty tomb and its open door once again. The curtain has been ripped. The rock has been rolled away. How can we say "no" as we are so free to say. . . "yes"? You see, I have pressed into the love relationship with God and the most amazing thing is that there are even more, greater, deeper, intimate moments of going from glory to glory. I have further to go and I find joy in knowing that there is more. I say "yes" to whatever He has for me. It is that easy. Yes, Lord! God promises that "Whether you turn to the right or to the left, your ears will hear a voice behind you, say, ' This is the way; walk in it'" (Isaiah 30:21 LAB). Press on and God will make all things new.

CHAPTER 9

Sharing in the Spirit

The most beautiful sharing there has been in my life is sharing in the Spirit. When people humble themselves and are vulnerable enough to share their hearts in relationship to their personal lives and their relationship with God, there is such an intimate connection of being one in the Spirit. The Bible tells us that "when two or more are gathered in Jesus name, there He is also." This is so true once we trust to just let go and try it. The following are some written dialogue opportunities I've had with others. I will keep details out of this writing for the sake of confidentiality and trust, but want to continue in the Spirit to share with you because I believe that the Lord has provided insights that may be helpful.

The woman that I am talking with is a Christian friend who truly loves and seeks the Lord, but who has found herself at times caught in strongholds that hold her captive. She represents any of us as we continue to grow and become free in the Lord. The dialogue actually appears more like an interview as I keep her details confidential:

My friend: Regarding the incest, how did you get to this place where you are so free? I think the answer is that I need to have more intimacy with God.

Me: With that question, I feel blessed to see you at a place spiritually where a door to freedom in Christ is beginning to be opened for you, as it was interesting to see how quickly you answered your own question. As you were sharing some about yourself, I thought of the time a few years ago that I felt so trapped within myself emotionally and wanted "out" so badly that I wanted to break the statue of a woman I have that sits on my coffee table. I wanted symbolically to free myself through that action. Instead, I found a therapist after a ten-year search that I trusted enough to share emotions with. Still, that therapeutic experience wasn't the entire answer as wholeness and freedom have since come through God alone as I have gone to Him with my feelings. That day you and I met was a first for me in not letting the enemy rob my testimony from me in a public place that consists of more than a few other people. Sharing so freely in front of a large group of people was new and exciting and even tiring as I was so plugged into God and the Holy Spirit and His purpose for me there! Praise God! What a blessing!

My friend: What the Lord revealed to me was that we have put up so many walls in so many areas of our lives that as they come down, we will be softer and healthier in different areas of our lives at different times. Praise the Lord! Then,

Joel 2:25 came to me, "God will repay us for the days the locust has eaten!" Then, the big question—do we really believe that God can and will heal us as we have had major damage? How big is our belief?? I think I finally believe it. I'm trying more and more to have more intimacy with the Lord and lean less on people. I'm beginning to think that intimacy is the key.

Me: We have to trust God as the One in control because, after all, He already is—no matter how much we try to take it from Him thinking somehow that we can do it better. It takes a lot of courage to open "Pandora's box" of emotions because once opened, your feelings begin pouring out and you may wonder if they will ever stop or if you will get through all of them. But you will, in His time—the perfect time suited to fit you. And God will be with you the whole way—not because I'm telling you so, but because He has made this promise to you. Those walls—they aren't bad things—you've just been outgrowing their purpose.

Be careful not to confuse the person who hurt you with the God who loves you. God is opening the door for your freedom because He wants it for you probably even more than you want it for yourself. As a matter of fact, He's already made the sacrifice so that you can claim the freedom. God is victorious! I believe that the walls are coming down. Don't force them; let them. God is good. Don't let the enemy cheat you from your freedom in God. Don't let the evil that has been done to you imprison you anymore. God's love won't fail you even though you may blame Him for the past pain. It wasn't Him. He won't hurt you too! I pray that you can trust Him, as He is the best Comforter and Counselor through the Holy Spirit that you can ever begin to imagine.

Let Him show you the way. His love never fails and He will assure you as you let Him draw you closer to Himself. The enemy will not like this, but keep your focus on the heavenly Father. He is the winner of this one already!

My friend: . . .What is God showing you?

Me: He is showing me that I don't need to be a certain way or conform to meet others' approval. He wants my obedience even if, like Noah, I act in ways strange to others—like building an ark too huge to move to water and standing nowhere near the river or sea. God has been helping me to write and to see that my writings are useful even in unpublished form. I feel like He is grooming me for something related to all of this writing. I'm seeing my own fears, and even though I am afraid, I will do as God wants me to anyway. God is showing me that He is my stronghold even when my own faith becomes shaky.

He is showing me that He loves me and has better dreams for my life than I could ever imagine or dream up for myself even when it doesn't appear like it. He is showing me that I need to stay focused on Him especially through the rough waters and even while His plans for me include my daughter moving so far away. The Lord is revealing His promises to me and showing me that He loves me, and His love is love that I can count on. He is showing me that I still have a lot to learn and that He will be with me throughout it all, as He will be with me for eternity. Thank you for asking. Praise God and feel His Holy Spirit upon you.

My friend: Your letter is so anointed that I made a copy and am carrying it with me. Maybe you could tell me a few things. I talked with a woman a couple of days ago who used to go to our church, and she said that it took her 3-4 years. She counseled with two different ministers at two different times. It's not that I am in a hurry, but I guess I feel that I have wasted a lot of time. I have been looking at these past problems for the past 15 years, and here I am, still looking for something more. I've read and read and read and counseled and been in a group, and then after that even led a group. Maybe I'm a "slow learner."

Me: There is a process led through faith by the heavenly Father, and the bottom line is the intimacy and surrendering to Him all the feelings similar to running like a child to a parent. There isn't a way around that, not that you are looking for one. Act on what and where you feel God is drawing you. That's as specific as I can be without knowing what you've been through.

My friend: What was the most significant thing in your healing?

Me: The most significant thing in my healing has been letting go and trusting God—taking all the feelings from the incest to Him and believing that He cares about my heart. It is this intimacy, trust, and focus (even when we have to go to Him and tell Him that we are incapable of having that intimacy without His help), that is vital in healing. It's okay to start wherever you are.

The most significant thing regarding my sense of freedom in Him was when I repented that I had allowed the incest to become a main focus and felt conviction that I had put it as a false god above the heavenly Father, failing to give Him first place in my life. I cried a lot of tears and felt His grace so completely. Also, I felt a sense of freedom when I decided that I would submit to Him using my situation to reach out in His most holy name through my testimony. You witnessed my moment of greatest freedom when I gave all that I had to follow Him by sharing my first public testimony. That was very hard for me because, like Moses, I don't see myself as an eloquent, or even a good, speaker. I really had to pray for God to give me the words to say and boldness that day.

My friend: How long did it take for you to heal?

Me: When I was trying to make the therapists and others into false gods, it was taking what seemed like forever. When I began to trust God, it took the time that I needed to find someone to hear me out and hold me when I became childlike and needed being held regarding the incest. I had never felt that motherly love at the depth that I needed. It took me 20 years after the abuse to find such a person. Perhaps the length of time had to do with the depth of pain, the ability of another to be able to go there with me, my readiness to trust that "darkness is as light to God" and to fall into the darkness relying on Him to catch me.

A few years later, I realized that I had made the sexual abuse a false god and that it was robbing me of my life and my testimony. It was approximately a year from that point until you met me giving my testimony publicly. This is also all within God's timing as to what He has going on in the bigger picture; and, He seems to be preparing me for something more. If I follow His timing and stop distracting myself with other things and keep from running in the opposite direction from Him because of my own fears, then His timing is the absolute perfect, soothing, healing, and freeing timing of all.

I feel His grace at this moment and it makes me cry with the overflowing of joy that I feel. Praise God! Praise You most Heavenly Father on high. To God be the Glory! Thank you, Jesus. Trust this anointing, my friend, because He wants you to have it and I want that for you too. Just let it happen. Let it be what it is. Praise God! Let Him be to you what He is, the Alpha and the Omega, the most merciful loving God. This letting my heart speak, where I just surrender to Him, is part of the uncensored writing that I was talking about earlier on.

My friend: How did you know when you were pretty much healed?

Me: How do you know when you are in love and have committed your life to someone?

My friend: I want to write my testimony or short life history to fill in the gaps for you. Maybe you won't accept all that I've done?

Me: (My friend shared with me personal things that are not mine to share. This writing of one's testimony is a good idea I think—whether it is shared or not.) I'm deeply sorry about what had happened to you. I'm also moved by all that you have shared. No, we don't all respond promiscuously, but many do. The enemy's deception was, as you said, your finding love or at least pleasure that tricked you into thinking it was love. Obviously, you were not responsible for what had happened to you as a child by the older person. Nor could you be in control as you were a little girl trying to piece together what was happening to you, and receiving "love" in whatever form was presented to you. You have really needed to think carefully to figure this out. Maybe if you can just think about it mentally without getting involved emotionally, then you won't have to feel the confusing mix of pain and sexual pleasure of those days either. The reason you beat yourself up in your effort to free your feelings also is clearer to me now. You may wonder if you even deserve to experience freedom.

Why wouldn't I accept you? I am a sinner. We are all lost souls, but by grace we are saved. Are you deserving? Am I? Absolutely not, except for this one reason, praise God: You are a child of God. That's the bottom line. You have already paid some serious consequences for your promiscuity. Is God's love really big enough for you and the sins you've committed? What a lot to sort out for an adult let alone a child. I'm sorry, but whether you feel anything or not, I do and I care. It's not too late for God to "restore the years the locust hath eaten, the cankerworm, and the caterpillar, and the palmerworm." It's not too late for you to "eat plenty, and be satisfied, and praise the name of the Lord your God that hath dealt wondrously with you" because God said it. He is speaking these words to your spirit because you are His child. This word of His is yours. He is saying it loud and clear. Praise God!

> Most merciful Father, thank you. Thank you more than my words can say. You know my heart and the joy I feel at what you have done, continue to do, and have given to each of us if we only receive it. Praise

121

God for our salvation and for new life in Him! Thank you, Jesus.

I feel Him and I get carried away. I'm not sorry at all. Oh Lord, what a high! Can you feel Him, too? Can you feel the anointing or is it just here? I want you to be able to touch these words and be touched by them and be able to experience His anointing, power, and grace, and goodness. His presence is lingering, so I have to praise Him more and more.

> Praise God! I praise You, heavenly Father, in Jesus name. Oh God, I don't care how nuts I sound. I pray for Your healing touch upon my friend. It is good. It is righteous. You are good and righteous! Let her feel Your love and Your grace for her. Oh Lord, give her the peace in her heart that goes beyond understanding. Take away that old sense of having to carry her own burdens and restore to her the years that the locusts have eaten, giving her the freedom that she deserves simply for being Your child—alive in You. Thank You, Lord, in Jesus' name. Amen.

I have never felt God so powerfully before in all of my writings, in my spirit, or in a room with hundreds of Christians. Thank you, my friend, for sharing. I'll write more tomorrow if anything comes to me that I should share with you. For now, I will include the following, which is what I've been writing to you tonight before receiving the message you sent to me. My heart is very open to you with much compassion. I hope you can let it in because it is a lot, but not even close to God's love for you. I pray that you can feel some sense of His love. Let it unfold at the pace that God is calling you to do so. Give yourself to Him. Feelings can't be forced. Change can't be forced. Healing can't be forced. Freedom can't be forced. The things that others do or don't do can't be forced. Take the pressure from yourself to get to these emotions and surrender them to God whether through spoken or written prayer. Let it go.

I've heard many sexual abuse stories. I have even heard ritual abuse stories. So, I care and I will continue to listen, but I don't want to add to your frustration and impatience with yourself or the pressure you are putting on yourself to feel something. I'm sincerely sorry if I've done that.

Also, I know that God sometimes gives me insights that touch very close to what is going on with others. I may not always be on target because I don't always 100% sort out me when God touches my heart with insights, but I know that I get close. I'm afraid that my participation has added to your being hard on yourself. So, I want to step back and pray simply that you feel God's grace, and that if nothing else, you recognize that I care, and have cared since the moment that I met you.

As for the things of your past, maybe you are as you say "digging up something that doesn't need to be dug up." If so, give it all to God and ask Him to take it and keep it. If it comes back, ask Him if you are the one taking it back from Him again and let Him know that you need Him to keep it even when you try to take it back. If you feel He wants you to look at the things of your past, ask Him to give you a peace about the direction you need to follow in order to grow closer to Him and be obedient to His plans for you. Then read your Bible, pray, sing songs of praise to Him, but mostly, listen expectantly and patiently. When things in the present upset you, continue running to the cross with those things as well.

My friend: It wasn't until I was in my late 30s when I thought I should explore if the abuse that I had suffered was causing problems with my attitudes, thoughts, feelings, lifestyle, etc. I never realized that it had set the tone for much of what I did, thought, and walls that I built. I began to read about the subject as I sought the Lord's direction. Again, I could give you all the details about the sexual abuse—but no feelings about it. I am much aware of the effects of the sexual abuse, even today. Again, I hope that I'm not looking for problems that I need not look for to feel "free in the spirit." I do know that grieving is a part of healing; and, obviously, I haven't grieved. I know what you say about "making" things happen. I cannot make my emotions surface, make anyone else change their behavior, make myself whole, or make myself be different. The Holy Spirit has to do the work, and I have to allow it. However, it is frustrating to me, making these realizations and not having emotions surface so that I can release them.

I know that I have been forgiven for all sin—past, present and future. I trust the Lord much more than ever before. I feel that to be victorious, I must live above my feelings. I must listen to the Word and live by it, not my feelings that change moment by moment. I momentarily realized yesterday as I re-read Joyce's (Joyce Meyer) information that I had some bad feelings right then that I didn't want to give up—another revelation. Occasionally now, when I share my story, people come onto me like I am down and out, haven't been healed at all, and reassure me that I need to stay in the

Word (of God), on my knees, and seek the Lord's direction, and I will get to where you are.

(I want to humbly interject in the midst of my friend's words that I've got further to go in my life—even regarding the incest and that where I overcome is only through God in my life.)

Well, I'm doing all that and praising the Lord, knowing that intimacy with the Lord is the answer to all. I still want to be freer and am not. Maybe I'm looking for fireworks and that's not happening. Most important, I would like to serve the Lord more freely. I would like to be more loving in His way, more people-oriented, more like Him. I want change because I don't want to continue making the same mistakes as I have in the past—I want to be more Christ-like. I hope you know that all this is bathed in prayer; the Lord is with me wherever I go. In whatever I do, I won't go alone. Give me your honest perspective.

Me: Am I healed from the sexual abuse? Yes! (This response is a claim to what Jesus did for me on the cross and reflects on the progress made.) Do I still have feelings and triggers regarding what my dad did to me? Yes, but they don't own me like they did before. I don't feel overpowered by them because of the way I've learned to go to God and let Him be victorious over them. I need to continue being free in sharing my story/testimony. Your frustration concerning your freedom is okay even if it doesn't feel good. We get frustrated and angry when we can't have what we want when we want it (now, yesterday, or 20 years ago). Frustration is an emotion. So, the best place to feel that frustration is in God's presence. We are back to this. (I say that lovingly and with a smile.) I'm not saying that you are not on your knees in prayer. You are telling me that you don't feel free, and I'm suggesting that you go to God with your feelings and lay them before Him like peeling an onion layer by layer. Don't confuse being lifted above your feelings as pretending you don't have them. I think the interpretation can get confusing as Christ certainly experienced His emotions as is evidenced in the Bible. Christians though— we get this idea that our walk, if done right, is to be without emotion. I disagree. Being lifted above your emotion is running to the cross with every single feeling even if you have no clue what it is about, and letting God lift you up as you give Him all of the Glory. You can't do that, but He can. What does holding onto the bad feelings do for you? What are you afraid of?

You answered your own questions to me about your frustrations with the asking of them. My going round and round with you will only serve to keep you stuck in your thoughts as you try to figure out all of the answers. Frustrated? Allow God to have it. Ask Him to take it as it is beyond your ability even to surrender it. Can you receive that from the heavenly Father?

Yes, I have had disagreements with my husband due to the abuse and how it affected my life. We also have had disagreements because of his "stuff." Everyone has "baggage." Everyone has places where God is working in their lives and seeking their faith and obedience in overcoming and growing closer to Him. Unfortunately, I was vulnerable to the assumption that the disagreements were often stemming back to my abuse—not that the incest didn't have negative (and positive—imagine that) impacts on our lives. They just weren't always to be the target of blame as that wasn't useful in getting us anywhere. My husband and I are very different—"complementary" is the term I like to use. We thought seriously of divorce twice, and then we dug in deeper and found more love. I'm so glad we did because we have since experienced a lot of blessings together that we would have missed out on. It took both of us plus our spiritual relationship with God, to make it through, growing in Him. So, yes, my life has been extremely affected by the abuse. I inventoried everything, analyzing like crazy, turning over every stone, feeling every feeling, getting frustrated when the feelings wouldn't come even though I could sense them lurking around inside of me, and suffering when the emotions became intense and my walls were too high to release them—as I once described as "like a bladder begging for a toilet when one is not available—I only need to cry." I'm now thankful for who I am as a result of what happened to me. Change it and miss out on all of the fun I've had? (smile)

Seriously, I love the people in my life and the path God has led me through as a result of the abuse. I love the depth of my life. I love the freedom that I have to play. I love the relationship I have with my family. I love the relationship I have with Jesus Christ, my Savior. Overcoming your feelings means going to Him and dumping everything and leaving it there. When you faithfully go to God (taking the focus away from being a better wife or mother or survivor of sexual abuse), when you release to Him every feeling rather than looking for the answers elsewhere like running to false gods, when you stop giving in to the enemy who is robbing you of your spiritual and emotional freedom (by keeping you focused on the frustration and staying stuck rather than the letting go); then, you will have all that you are looking for. That is what dying to self and letting Jesus shine through you is all about.

A healthy family? I don't know what that is exactly supposed to look like. A close one in the Bible is Joseph, Mary and Jesus. Of the three, perfection could only be found in Jesus; but quite honestly, I wonder what Mary felt about Him when He expressed a "temper tantrum" in the temple. I may have been embarrassed even if the people were wrong, and I may have scolded Him asking Him to behave more "respectfully" in God's house. What do I know? (smile)

I do know that this communication is bathed in prayer or you wouldn't be able to ask for my honest perspective. Rather, you would be persecuting me for getting even close to giving it. He is with you wherever you go, in whatever you do and you aren't alone ever. God bless you!

You can't move from one level of healing or freedom to another just because you or a loved one wants it. If you could, you would have done it. But, if someone's expectations discourage or upset you, you may need time alone to pray, go to the living Word, and respond rather than react or get caught up in that same old dance. If it is your problem, change it; but if it isn't yours, then just stand still firmly and lovingly and let the other person deal or not deal with their problem. Act as God leads you. Don't expect to change the other person, but respond to another with respect. Choose time to talk with them when they are mutually good. We all have "sore/soar" spots where Satan can use others to keep us paralyzed rather than progressing. Remember God is victorious. When we come face to face with the sore place, He will provide for us (in His time and His way) to soar above whatever the problem is. If the problem is about expectations, we can go to God directly and talk to Him (aligning ourselves with His expectations of us). Our intimacy with Him will help as we see Him in our lives each day. We can write about how we have seen God working in our lives and refer back to those writings as reminders in difficult moments. We can keep a record of how we have experienced victory in Him.

Heavenly Father, I ask that You reveal Yourself deeper and deeper to each of us everyday. Set our steps with Your pace, help us keep our eyes on You, and remember Your promise in Joel 2:25 as we know that time is on our side. Help us to receive Your promise with our palms open and upward. There is time, Father. We have forever in You even as this fast-paced world and the number of years You have given us to live here try to trick us into thinking otherwise. Lord, you know the plans you have for our lives and the purpose you have for us. Let us rest in your arms, trusting in your ways. I also ask that You, Almighty God and King of Kings, reveal to us our victory in you as you bind and cast out the power that others' expectations have on us to grow and change. Release in us comfort and confidence that you are restoring what the locusts have eaten. In Jesus most Holy and Blessed name. Thank you, Father. I love you. Amen.

(Please take the time now to stop, read and meditate prayerfully on Proverbs 3:5-6, then continue by asking yourself the following question which I asked my friend.)

How are you with the stuff I've given feedback about? I hope I have handled your vulnerable sharing well. I mean that sincerely. There's a lot I have to learn yet, so I worry about the effects of my "honest perspective" on others. I really care about people and that is why I throw my heart and soul into what I'm doing. God bless you.

My friend: Yes, I do have an urgency to understand. But I can't say that I have an urgency to understand rather than stay with the feeling. I will keep my eyes on the little successes and praise God for them. I sure do appreciate the feedback and new insights and perspectives.

My group started up again. The leader wanted me to go to a counselor for a one-time visit after I told the group (many times) that I just don't feel anything. I told him that I had told my story several times. He said that I may have pushed the feelings downward—instead of taking them to Christ for release. The other counselor wants us to throw out all the psychology we ever learned. He says that stuff isn't in the Scriptures.

Me: (I was also asked about personality-type tests.) I think of personality tests as mind games that cause a sense of perfectionism and confusion based upon someone's perception of what is the right way to be and what isn't. What do the tests really matter anyway if you are walking with the Holy Spirit and acting in accordance with His will? I'm being blunt because I've been there. Hebrews 4:12 helps me sort through all of those manmade dead end roads and categorical, dehumanizing distractions. Healing comes to us by God through spiritual intimacy and faith within His timing. I do agree with the counselor that talking about the experiences of abuse may have caused you to push the feelings downward. I believe getting into and possibly stressing yourself out about the personality tests also serve to push the feeling downward. As for the temperaments, I'm not sure why that is so important. I agree with the counselor who says to throw the psychology away. The truth will set you free, not the facts.

I suppose that to use the Bible as a psychological tool, it would be best for you to turn to the character whom you most feel like you have something in common with. Feel it out with them. I think you do have feelings that you aren't aware of about the abuse. The more truthful way to describe what is going on with you could be to share that you have feelings that aren't surfacing yet. (That's a slight shift from "I just don't feel anything.") Share that you want to be open to those feelings when they do come; and you may talk about what you need from those in your group should you have some feelings during group time. You may want to explore what those feelings could be like and the kinds of responses or space or special care that you think you may need when you feel them. You may also want to be attentive to how your body feels. You may talk about any tightening, tension, or knots—not to analyze them, but to share what is going on in your body. You may, for example, feel something in the pit of your stomach and talk through what you feel, possibly noticing a shifting or the feeling possibly moving upward. You may even want to talk about or journal what that feeling would say. Be creative as to what your tightness in your chest or heart or lump in your throat might say. This is just an idea because I think you've put so much pressure on yourself regarding not feeling that I think your feelings need to find a safe place.

A sense of safety includes your surroundings, the support of those around you, and whether or not you are going to treat the tender feelings as if they need lots of gentleness and love. I think that I'd avoid anyone that encourages your going further into psychologizing yourself or doing any cognitive anything because talking through your experience without very slowly and prayerfully touching the heart of each thought/memory/sensation in your body may cause your feelings to be pushed downward. It's amazing what the body remembers over the years and how our feelings are reflected physically. I see your feelings like a baby growing inside of you until they are ready to be born. When the time is right, you will hear the baby's cry. That cry is what you need to prepare yourself to nurture.

I'll conclude this discussion here even as it continues past and present. I've chosen these conversations because they relate to the topic of my writings overall regarding childhood sexual abuse, therapy, and God's desire, ability and promise to deliver us and set us free so that we may have life more abundantly. Sharing in the Spirit through writing is wonderful. Sharing in the Spirit in person is even better. I love being so open spiritually with others. More recently I have opened myself and trusted God in allowing His comfort through hours of praying with and prayer from a friend who I am thankful for. She has prayed for me in the areas of my life where I have needed deeper healing. God is a God of restoration.

Such a relationship is about risk. I once wrote to this friend, 'Trust is not always an easy word for me. It is not easy for me to share my heart and my tears or open up; it is not easy to kick off my shoes, remove my socks and let you anoint my feet; it is not easy to let you touch me with God's love for me. It is not easy, but once we are in those secret places of my heart and mind, it is so very lovely, healing and moving. It is so very nice. I hug you now and say that God is so very wonderful, perfect, all knowing and faithful. I love Him. I love you.

As for the topic of freedom: We are free to do what we want; quickly losing sight of the One who sets us free. In our search to create our own panacea, we can lose sight of the one and only Cure-all who gives us freedom. Through God's grace, we can always refocus and begin anew, finding our freedom for the first time or once again, in Him. Thinking about the anointed prayer time with my friend who prays with and for me, I think of that time like joyfully being childlike on a swing moving back and forth. I feel the warm fresh breeze from the motion blowing back my hair and cooling my body on a hot summer day. In prayer, we step backward for momentum then thrust ourselves forward. Again and again, we try to touch the sky with our feet as we feel the freedom of movement and the air all around us. Then, we sit back and let it just happen until we are ready to touch the earth again and know even as the swing stops in the same place where we started it that we have been somewhere.

That's how it is to share so beautifully, innocently and intimately in the Spirit of the Living God. We may have to stop and take care of the daily details of our lives, but always there is the joy of knowing that there is another place to be, there is such an awesome holy place that the Lord has for us and we know individually and in unity that we've been somewhere. We've been in the freedom of the Spirit of the Lord.

This refreshing place of freedom is one I can tell you about only with limited words, but here is my prayer for you: Surrender to Jesus, ask Him to forgive you for the times you have turned away, tell Him what you feel in your heart, ask Him to open you to receive more of Him and His love, rest in His loving arms, lay everything else down and praise Him. Believe His promises for you and His Word that God inhabits our praises. Receive Him. Talk to others about Him. Share in His Spirit. Experience His freedom. In Jesus' holy name, I pray. Amen.

CHAPTER 10

Bridging the Gap

Not by might nor by power, but by my Spirit, says the Lord Almighty (Zechariah 4:6 LAB).

s you can see throughout these pages, I knew all along the way, the truth, and the life; but in my pain, I got off track with manmade "close, but not quite there" alternatives. Unfortunately, "not quite there" is still a dead end road. We are in this world, but not of it; so, how in this world, but through the power of the Holy Spirit, can we survive such a dilemma as that?

The Son of God came to us and was made flesh. In human form, Jesus was not above seeking out the Father in prayer through the power of the Holy Spirit. As Jesus was preparing to fulfill His purpose of taking our sins upon Himself by going to the cross, He prepared His disciples with the promise of another "counselor." In John 14:15-19, Jesus spoke these words:

> *If you love me you will obey what I command. And I will ask the Father, and He will give you another Counselor to be with you forever—-the Spirit of truth. The world cannot accept Him, because it nei-ther sees Him nor knows Him. But, you know Him, for He lives with you and will be in you. I will not leave you as orphans; I will come to you. Before long, the world will not see me anymore, but you will see me. Because I live, you also will live* (LAB).

Further, Jesus told the disciples in Acts 1:8 that they would "receive power when the Holy Spirit comes on (them) and they will be His witnesses. . .to the ends of the earth" (LAB).

> Oh Holy Spirit, I need you. I need you so much right now. I feel God calling me to write and yet I don't know what to say. Oh merciful God, what should I say? Please lead me in Jesus' name. Amen.

We know that sin separated us from God. We know that the only way to the Father is through the Son as we believe in the Lord Jesus Christ, bow down before Him, and praise His name. We know that Jesus took our sins upon Himself and died on a cross. We Christians, as followers of Jesus Christ, know (to such a minimal degree that does not compare in any way) what it is like to take on the sins of others. We know that others paid some of the consequences when Jonah did not obey God's command to go to Nineveh and preach against the wickedness there. Instead Jonah ran away (as we often "try" to do, but who can flee from the om-nipresence of the Almighty God?). Jonah boarded a ship and "the Lord sent a great wind on the sea, and such a vio-lent storm arose that the ship threatened to break up." The sailors were afraid and cried out to their own gods. They cast lots to see who was responsible for this calamity and the lot fell to Jonah. The sailors knew that Jonah was run-ning away from the Lord and they wanted to know what he had done. "The sea was getting rougher and rougher" causing everyone on board to suffer for what Jonah had done. Of course, God used the consequences of Jonah's dis-obedience as an example of the triumphant Lion's unmatch-able, unbeatable, and unstoppable power. In His perfect plan, God turned the others away from false gods and onto Himself. The men threw Jonah overboard, and immediately "the raging seas grew calm. At this the men greatly feared the Lord, and offered a sacrifice to the Lord and made vows to Him."

We know something of what it is like to receive portions of the consequences of others' sins. Our experience is only minimal, though, because Jesus took it all. So, we can bridge the gap between our Creator and us only through our faith in the risen Savior, our Lord Jesus Christ. We even know that it is the Holy Spirit who guides us to the Bridge of Life Everlasting—the Beloved Son of The Almighty Father. Yet, do we know who it is that bridges the gap between the religion of psychology and God? Who is it that bridges the gap between whatever else we may set our sights upon while dodging the risk required in getting to the Alpha and the Omega? Believing in Jesus is one thing; but if I cross that bridge to the Father, He may just ask me to take a good look at the Living Water and jump in. Then, while in that immersion of the deep blue sea, a whale may swallow me up. And what if He doesn't spit me out? Or what if he spits me out somewhere out there in the middle of nowhere? Then, what do I do? I may have to die to myself, out there in the middle of nowhere, in order to be born again in Christ. I may have to surrender to the power and guidance of God through the Living Water that waits to engulf me. And, Who is that One who wants control of my life? Who is that supposed Comforter and Counselor upon whom I am to rely upon for an eternity of out there somewhere in the middle of nowhere? Who is it that bridges the gap between the religions of the intellect and the Risen Savior? Who bridges the gap between the King of Kings and us?

Here's the good news that I get to tell you about: "From inside the fish, Jonah prayed to the Lord his God." He cried out these words,

> *You hurled me into the deep, into the very heart of the seas, and the currents swirled about me (out there somewhere in the middle of nowhere). . . . Then, (Jonah) said, 'I have been banished from your sight; yet I will look again toward your holy temple.' . . . To the roots of the mountains I sank down. . . but you brought my life up from the pit, O Lord my God. . . . Those who cling to worthless idols forfeit the grace that could be theirs. But I, with a song of thanksgiving, will sacrifice to you. What I have vowed I will make good. Salvation comes from the Lord* (Jonah 2:3-10 LAB).

And here is more good news: "And the Lord commanded the fish, and it vomited Jonah onto dry land" because, you see, there is no such place to the One who created all places (even to the depths of the oceans and the belly of whales), as "out there somewhere in the middle of nowhere." The place otherwise known to us as where we are when we ignore the call of the Holy Spirit and, instead, we follow our own direction. So, what happened to Jonah once on dry land? He went to Nineveh. God saved Jonah, the sailors, and the people of Nineveh. We need not forfeit our grace to self-will because God will surely find us and encourage us to obey His plan and purpose for us as Jonah learned so well.

We know that sin separated us from God. We know that the only way to the Father is through the Son as we believe in the Lord Jesus Christ, bow down before Him, and praise His name. We know that Jesus took our sins upon Himself and died on a cross. We know that the third day, He arose from the dead and ascended into heaven. We know that He has provided Himself as the bridge to our salvation and everlasting life. So; I share about the Holy Spirit, as I ask Him to guide me in these writings, because we suffer on this earth. We suffer because it is difficult here. It is so difficult here that God created therapists, ministers, psychologists, theologians, and lots of people to help us along the way. Still, let us be sure to bridge the gaps that remain.

Our study of human behavior and the Bible is nothing without a relationship with the Father, the Son, and the other Bridge—the Holy Spirit who comes upon us that we may witness for Jesus as He becomes alive in us and we are made new. Let us not forget to welcome into our lives the One who leads us home to Jesus. Let us not underestimate the power of God through the Holy Spirit. Rather, let us take a good look at the Living Water and jump right in to be filled out there somewhere in the middle of nowhere where our loving God is in control. The heavenly Father will quench our thirst. If in God we trust, in Him we will be satisfied. In Him, fountains of living water will flow from out of our bellies for His name's sake and to the glory of God forever.

Faith

To walk with God through the guidance of His Holy Spirit is a powerful movement of faith. Yet, faith is such a huge topic, how do I capture the words to share about it here? Even Jesus has said to us in the midst of the fearful waves "ye men (and women) of little faith." We look for leaders to "walk the talk." We look to leaders to walk the faith walk, and if we see that it works for them (as we watch through microscopic lenses too often seeking to criticize in an excuse not to try), well then maybe we will try it too. Or maybe not this time, but the next time. Yes, we promise, the next time we will allow ourselves to feel the Holy Spirit nudging us—the next time!

As I look over my life, I have sought God's strength in walking in His way because no one can do it without Him. As I look back, I can see so much pain and suffering in my life and the lives of others. I have seen so many extremes of suffering. Along with my own experiences with incest, the persecution from others for trying to follow my beliefs, and the beating up of my mom and brothers by my dad, I have also listened firsthand to many painful stories of rape, incest, and ritual abuse. I have seen the switching of personalities in a beautiful young woman managing to cope with her horrid life, dealt with abused children removed from their families and placed with unknown parental figures, watched elderly persons being given shock treatments (one crying out "what have I come to?"), a needle stuck in another to get her blood pressure down and a lead vest placed on yet another woman to protect her regarding something to do with her pacemaker. I have also seen my brother after he had been nearly murdered needlessly by a police officer. I have seen how drugs and alcohol tear apart lives and families, the devastation of a youth group/Sunday school friend killing the father of another friend, the agony of my pregnant mother crying that my dad "pushed" her down the cellar steps, the trauma of a man with a knife wound in his stomach entering my home with blood spilling onto my carpet, and the deception of a police officer in uniform obtaining information from me only to pistol whip the man he was seeking. I have seen a lot.

Sometimes, as when I saw my pregnant mom crying after my dad had pushed her down the cellar steps when I was three years old, I remember literally being outside of myself in shock and dismay. I watched myself walk around my mom sitting on the floor as I looked to understand what happened, see how she hurt, and see how I could care for her. I remember observing myself observing the situation. Yet, while I have seen a lot of pain, I have also seen a lot of love.

I have witnessed the love of people going out of their way to help others and experienced the anointing of people in prayer for one another. I have had valued people love me and I have loved them so much that my heart overflowed with joy. I have treasured the miracle of my children being born and placed in my arms for the first time. Other times I have soaked in the sights of beautiful sunsets and oceans with seagulls, the wonders of Niagara Falls, and a large cross on a mountainside. I have enjoyed my children growing, laughing, playing, sleeping and cherished my husband holding my hand, my mother hugging me, and the birth of my first grandchild. I have immersed myself in singing songs of praise with others and God's anointing touch upon me. I have seen a lot. I can look at my experiences from many angles and depths. I can become withdrawn in thought like a flower that closes at the trace of darkness, or I can open brightly like that same flower at the first peek of daylight. In the depths of some of my inward journeys, I can feel very lonely even as I read the Bible and have some prayer time. That is when I know it is time to open up and reach out again in Christian love and fellowship.

One day, though, I was feeling the loneliness of being in a new area for our Christmas, and, at the same time, it was my oldest daughter's first Christmas away from us. There were a few weeks to wait for the activities I had gotten involved in to start back up again after the holidays. From within that secret place, I thought of many of the things I have seen and stayed there without words to anyone about my thoughts. I felt drawn to that place, I suppose, like Jesus in the garden of Gethsemene. As I look again at all that I have seen in my life, I think of the little feet that my friends made for me. Attached to them is a verse that says "Walk by faith, not by sight" (2 Corinthians 5:7).

I "see" a woman go out of her way to walk down a dirt and gravel alley just to ask a little girl, "Do you know God?" I can only imagine what was going on inside this woman when the Holy Spirit led her out of her path and down that alley. Whatever she thought, whatever she saw, whatever had come before in her life, the woman chose to walk by faith. She came to me as a vessel led by the Holy Spirit, so that I could receive eternal life through Jesus Christ. I'm still learning to know God. It's a lifelong journey in which I will see many more things, but I will always remember the woman who, through faith, let me see hers. To walk with God through the guidance of His Holy Spirit is a powerful movement of faith.

Oh heavenly Father, please continue to guide us in our walk of faith. Strengthen and comfort us as we take steps down alleys away from the convenient paths we planned. Give us the courage and boldness to actualize the words You whisper to us. Help us to follow through when we say "Thy will be done." Glory to God in the highest and to whom I pray in Jesus' name. Amen.

CHAPTER 11

Moses Speaks

In Exodus chapter 3, we see faith at work through Moses. God appeared to Moses in the form of a burning bush saying

> *I have indeed seen the misery of my people in Egypt. I have heard them crying out because of their slave drivers, and I am concerned about their suffering. So I have come down to rescue them from the Egyptians and to bring them up out of that land into a good and spacious land, a land flowing of milk and honey. . . . And now the cry of the Israelites has reached me, and I have seen the way the Egyptians are oppressing them. So now, go. I am sending you to Pharaoh to bring my people the Israelites out of Egypt* (LAB).

Moses then asked God, "Who am I, that I should go to Pharaoh and bring the Israelites out of Egypt?" God replied,

> *I will be with you. And this will be the sign to you that it is I who have sent you: When you have brought the people out of Egypt, you will worship God on this mountain.*

Then, in Exodus 4:10 Moses said to the Lord, "Oh Lord, I have never been eloquent, neither in the past nor since you have spoken to your servant. I am slow in speech and tongue" (LAB). The Lord replied, "Who gave man his mouth? . . .Is it not I, the Lord? Now go; I will help you speak and will teach you what to say." Moses persisted, "Please send someone else to do it." God became angry because Moses felt so inadequate that he was unable to trust God to help him speak. So, God sent Moses' brother, Aaron, to help saying,

> *I know (Aaron) can speak well. . . .You shall speak to him and put words in his mouth; I will help both of you speak and will teach you what to do. He will speak to the people for you, and it will be as if he were your mouth and as if you were God to him* (Exodus 4:14-16 LAB).

I love this scripture; and I love the fact that Moses' sense of inadequacy about speaking and God's response is important enough to record in the Bible because I have such a difficult time speaking. Fearing that I may have to speak, I've struggled with the success of completing this writing. The fact that what I have to talk about involves freedom from captivity due to the sensitive subject of childhood sexual abuse doesn't help. I struggle to find the words to describe my heart and that is the very reason I write. My words get lost in my brain plenty of times even when I'm talking casually to friends and family. I even struggle to focus on what messages to leave on answering machines. And, of course, my friends lovingly tease me. . . . So, here's something I wrote:

After the Beep

I called you, not really knowing what to say. I took a breath to say hello, hoping that the message would come in the midst of our words together. It seems I never really know what to say. I keep trying to stop my will from getting between my words and you. I hear you answer, or at least it is your voice. So, I try to formulate the words to be recorded. I will not be able to go back to change, erase, or start them over again. Somehow, writing seems safer. But then, words on paper seem so permanent—freezing me in one place. Now, I hear the beep. It is the long intrusive kind where my message swirls around in my head as the dissonant tones screech into my ear. Quickly, I clear my throat and take a breath (those sounds I do not wish to have recorded). Hearing the silence, I know it is my turn to speak. But; I don't know how. "God help me to say what you would have me say," I pray as my will slips away. How is it that it seems some people have so much to talk about? Where is it that they get those words? How do they retain such intelligent information? Having learned that there isn't really much time between the end of the beep and the silence's insistence that I speak (or don't), I ramble on. Simultaneously; I pray that God speaks through me. After all, after the beep. It is His wisdom I want to impart, His words I want to say, His love I want to share, His words I want to give. . .to you. . . .Whatever it was, whatever it is, I've said it now—no going back. Messy, sloppy, divine, sweet, loving, or none of the above; I hang up the receiver and wait. On His timeline, . . . we proceed. . . .

About the time I wrote "After The Beep," a friend invited me to give a few minutes of my testimony to about 400 people. Despite my fears, I believed God was calling me to share, so I had to obey. The following is some of what God helped me say about my spiritual growth at that time. There were some spontaneous thoughts, but I actually read a lot. Still, I prayed for courage and boldness. God was so good! There are four areas of my life in which I have grown:

First, God has helped me shrink my will in obedience to His.

Second, God has helped me to become more intimate with Him. I received Christ into my heart and asked Him to be in charge of my life at age 10. Imagine my salvation as my having received a bar of soap. I even bathed with it through church life, fellowship, worship, and prayer. Lately, though, I have found a deeper intimacy filled with joy and praise and because I have the soap, I'm bathing with it, and my water is the Living Water.

God provided us with the Holy Spirit to guide us, strengthen us, comfort us, intercede in prayer for us, counsel us, change our hearts, remain present within us, heal us, and baptize us. He births in us a new mind and new life in God as we seek the truth that sets us free, repent and receive

God's grace. Praise God! I have increased my interaction with God and discovered deeper intimacy with Him. It is a great blessing to be able to turn to God, our heavenly Father, every second of every day and know that He is with us and for us. He loves us and sent His Son to die for us and rose again so that we may have eternal life! What joy I feel in becoming more intimate with our Creator! Praise God!

Third, I have learned to focus more on God by trusting Him with my burdens and not taking them back (as if I can handle them better than He can). I have learned to "be still and know that He is God," to pace myself in daily activity, and to rise above everything through "walking by faith and not by sight." These have all been lessons for me to practice. I have kept my eyes on Him like Peter walking to Jesus on the water, and He has remained faithful. I have been learning to give my emotions to Him, running to Him like a child to a parent. Focusing on God as my heavenly Father has been a healing that He has brought me through difficult times over the past several years because I had deeply painful experiences with my earthly father. I felt devastated when, at age 14, my dad sexually abused me. Then, again, I felt devastated when, at age 22, my dad died and we were unable to have a resolution of the matter. I know I am not alone in having been sexually abused by a parent or parental figure in childhood. There are many who know first hand something of what I am talking about. Statistics say one in four. At a recent gathering of Christian women, there were 3 out of 6.

To heal from the trauma, I sought emotional support in workshops, self-help books, a degree in Psychology, helping others, church, food, and therapy. I ran to all of the socially acceptable things that I thought would save me from my own wanting to die. The therapists I saw were as helpful as they could be. None could be the false gods that I had tried to make them into. With each loss, I was getting heavier and heavier. My focus on healing became a false god. My focus on my dad's death and the emptiness I felt became a false god. My focus on (and I say this with great compassion and sensitivity, but I have to say it because it is the truth) sexual abuse became a false god. The love and the other blessings of keeping my focus on God were being robbed from me. I was like the woman that had been bleeding for 12 years going from doctor to doctor to heal when at last, through faith, she reached out and touched the hem of Jesus' cloak and was healed. Some therapists and several sexual abuse survivors said that it wasn't necessary to forgive my dad. But God told me to forgive so that I may be forgiven, judge not lest I be judged, and ye without sin cast the first stone. I love my parents. I forgive them. I honor my parents with this testimony, as God is victorious! He alone frees hearts from captivity. He reigns over all things. He has conquered evil. He is our hope and our salvation. He is the sovereign God. I have been starving for Him and He has filled me. Praise God! May He forever be my focus and yours.

Fourth, I have been learning to make a deeper commitment to God by sharing openly about Him. One way this happened was when I was leading a Christian study group. Doing so meant that I would have to open my heart more fully to others regarding God's place in my life, and I would even have to pray out loud in the presence of others. Throughout my life, I have felt a sense of isolation, but I have learned that God will never leave me nor forsake me. I have also learned to like myself for one very important reason: I am a child of God! As God's child, I won't allow the one who came to steal, kill, and destroy to rob me of my testimony. Today, I am here in obedience to God. I am speaking out in the faith of God's love for me and in His plan for my life. This is my humble commitment to His will and His presence in my life. Thanks be to God, and thank you.

Something happened to me during the time I was speaking to the group of nearly 400 participants. Somehow, I did not care what anyone thought of me. After all, I was claiming God and I felt His presence ever so close. I experienced Him in the boldness of what He was speaking through me in obedience to Him. I felt my weakness, yet I felt His strength. While risking the possible poor opinion of others, I felt God's love. I walked toward my seat and felt the hug of the woman who had organized the day. She and I still had our connection—Jesus. She whispered something in my ear about how my words had needed to be shared.

The following week after that special day was Mother's Day. As I was thanking my daughter for the stuffed frog she gave as my Mother's Day gift, I was feeling God's hands were on this particular gift. My daughter told me that she "remembered that I liked frogs and used to have a stuffed frog." I had won the frog she was referring to at an amusement park. I typically don't waste money on those games, but that day I saw the frog and felt that it was to be mine. I played the game once and took the frog home. This same daughter that was about five or six years old at the time (now age 23), placed a piece of her own jewelry on the frog and named it "Hug Me." The reason "Hug Me" was so important was because in my early counseling sessions with the first therapist, she started choking and said to excuse her because she "had a frog in her throat." I playfully had this vision of a frog in her throat and my pulling it out. So, I went to the store and bought a small, plastic, wind-up frog that can swim in water. I gave the frog to the first therapist. Later, in my efforts to let her go, I offered her a small package of "crumbled cookies" in exchange for the frog. I wound up the frog and freed it in the creek that branched off from a nearby river. It was a cute exchange. I gave her the cookies and she swam the little frog playfully over to me in mid-air. That is when things were good between us.

When things were not so good and I was moving to a town near where I grew up, and trying to lovingly say good-bye, I left "Hug Me" in a brown lunch bag near her office door. I don't know what ever happened to that little frog. I just know that here I am with this new frog that my daughter gave me, spending my Mother's day at one of my favorite places—an amusement park, noticing a frog painted on the side of a radio station van that happened to be at the park, looking at a huge Ferris wheel and remembering the lunch that she and I once had where we talked about amusement parks. I told her I was afraid that if I rode a Ferris wheel with her that she would rock it. I remembered that she assured me that she wouldn't.

As is common in my relationship with the first therapist, these kinds of things often happened. I was no more in control of these little "God-incidences" than I was in control of being on the highway with my family once so long ago and seeing her driving beside me. She suddenly zoomed off at the exit and I didn't understand. Now I wonder if the God-incidence frightened her as if I had planned the chance meeting. God seems to work in my life that way. I never wanted to move to that county where she worked any more than I had wanted to move (more recently) to this area where she had once lived. I wanted to be in my hometown area all along! Still, I am here and I think back to those days when I was there remembering how much my field of study, psychology, went against the grain of my Christian faith. My goal was to face and heal the wounds within my life so that I could help heal the wounds in the hearts of others. The first therapist told me I was too "sensitive and caring" to be her friend. I never understood because every time I would close the door, it would somehow keep opening, so I would write and write. And, here I am still writing.

It was at that campus I received a third place writing award for a paper I wrote in my Social Psychology class. What the professor instructed me to write about went against the grain for me, so I wrote it differently and backed up the story with supporting research. I risked failing the test, but I had to do it that way in support of my own sense of what was right. God came through for me. I received an "A" along with a certificate and $50 through the campus-wide writing contest. I was so nervous to receive the award that I became too stressed out to go to my Stress Management class. Instead, I walked up and down the hallway praying. I made it through. Praise God! You see, there is a peace that passeth beyond understanding. The relaxation techniques were side tracking for me. It's like all the self-esteem building that therapists focus on. I worked to apply those strategies, but the bottom line is that I am a child of God. Being His is the thing that matters most, the thing I like myself for, the thing that allows me to fly no matter what as God continues to draw me closer to Him.

Some Christian family and friends expressed concern about my participation in the field of psychology. Some have watched my pain increase through my search down that road. I love reading Mark 5:25-34. Read the verses for yourself, and understand their concerns. I "had suffered a great deal under the care of many doctors and had spent all (I) had, yet instead of getting better (in ways, I) grew worse" (LAB). In addition to this Goliath, I was going against the grain that caused some therapists to further analyze me, be annoyed with me, and try to set me straight. These people are experts at analysis and using their authority and much research in the field to create change. I felt as though they were trying to psychologically destroy me as I stood for what I believed.

I wonder why God took me down this road of psychology when my experiences often went against the grain. I think of Moses again and how he was raised in Egypt. In Acts 7:20-44, Luke writes a speech given by Stephen regarding Moses and Jewish history.

> . . .*Moses was born and he was no ordinary child. For three months he was cared for in his father's house. When he was placed outside (to protect him from being murdered—see your Bible for more about this part of the life of Moses), Pharaoh's daughter took him and brought him up as her own son. Moses was educated in all of the wisdom of the Egyptians and was powerful in speech and action* (LAB).

Moses is said to have been educated and powerful in speech and action, yet he felt he did not have eloquent speech and

153

asked God to choose someone else to free God's people, the Israelites, from captivity and slavery in the land of Egypt. Even Jesus came to live on earth as man before His plan, to set us free from sin, was fulfilled. The purpose God had for Moses was to connect with Pharaoh and to be educated and raised in Egypt, so that Moses could fulfill God's purpose and carry out God's plan for his life. Moses was set apart from God's people, the Israelites from whom Moses was born, so that he could set them free from the oppression of slavery in Egypt. In the midst of these two worlds, as a person connected to both of them with a mission given by God that was greater than himself, there is little wonder to me, at least, that Moses did not feel he had eloquent speech.

What can be said about the position you have between two worlds that are very much a part of your life, yet are in ways very opposed to one another? What a dilemma. According to the book of Acts,

> *When Moses was 40 years old, he decided to visit his fellow Israelites. He saw one of the Israelites being mistreated by an Egyptian, so he went to his defense and avenged him by killing the Egyptian. Moses thought that his own people would realize that God was using him to rescue them, but they did not. The next day Moses came upon two Israelites who were fighting. He tried to reconcile them by saying, "Men, you are brothers; why do you want to hurt each other?" but the man who was mistreating the other pushed Moses aside and said "Who made you ruler and judge over us?" Moses fled and it took 40 more years until he heard from God that "I (God) have indeed seen the oppression of my people (the Israelites) in Egypt. . . .Now come,*

I will send you back to Egypt. This is the same Moses who they had rejected with their words, "Who made you ruler and judge?"

Moses was sent to be their ruler, judge, and deliverer by God Himself for He led them out of Egypt.. . .

I am not saying that I am anyone's ruler or judge. I am saying that I have experienced two worlds with a purpose and plan that God has for my life and that it is hard. Educated or not, sometimes there seems to be no eloquent words to speak in this place where I write, seeking to allow God to use me. This is a place where I am to set captives free (including myself) from the pain of childhood sexual abuse and possibly other strongholds that keep people from experiencing freedom in the Lord. Counseling has its purpose as well, yet I'm not in the same place, or mindset, as psychology alone would have me be. I stand in a gap between a field that, like Jesus, also seeks to set captives free and heal the brokenhearted. From within this gap, I navigate both arenas, and I seek the Lord to help make a bridge for His people to His own heart. In alignment with my heart's desire, I stand as firmly as possible on solid ground and the truths of God's Word. I have slipped at times when I haven't been faithful to seek God's way, but I know that no one comes to the Father except through the Son. God alone is ultimately our healer and deliver. I walk in the authority, through Jesus, over the enemy as Moses did, demanding, "Let my people go!"

It is one thing to go against the grain in the medical field, but another thing to try and survive a decade of challenging the minds of those who dissect your brain ad manipulate your emotions to get you into a more manageable norm. It's a wonder I've made it here to tell you about it. But God was with me, and I turned to Him and thought, "If I just touch His clothes, I will be healed." And He said, "Daughter, your faith has healed you. Go in peace and be freed from your suffering." Praise God!

There is a danger in giving the manmade field of psychology too much power. That is why I assert the importance of building a bridge between psychology and the wholeness and the freedom found in God alone. There is an acceptance in the field for people who are not in obedience to God to build upon lifestyles opposed to God. A therapist saying that something is okay doesn't make it okay. The client receives the temporary fix and builds on that "house upon the sand." Instead, we need to build a bridge to the way, the truth and the life. No one goes to the Father except by Jesus. The truth will set us free within the wide love-filled boundaries of God as is written in His word, the Living Word. Build the bridge. Better yet, stay faithful to the Almighty Counselor of counselors and He, being faithful to you, will build it for you. Praise God!

I have had special relationships with therapists. I love them and the work they do very much. I believe God works through them. I also believe that my receiving the writing award was through my obedience to God. I believe that He has drawn me to the first counselor and the field of psychology even when, in my own will, I closed the doors or others closed the doors on me. I believe that it has been God bringing me through all the trauma and healing, in His name and to His glory, as I have made a comparison between spirituality and psychology, however different or intertwined they may be.

We need to not be so quick to pigeon hole anyone into having certain psychological disorders or issues, but instead, to build the bridge. As for me, Jesus has built my bridge. Sometimes I know that He will have me do things and say things in accordance with His will that do not agree with worldly ideas. I love Him and others as He commanded, so I have to have faith and write and speak as He has commissioned me to. Sometimes my words and actions do not appear life enhancing from a psychological perspective, but what matters is that it is from God. Now, I don't know what all these frogs in my life are about. Maybe it is God's way of still saying "let my people go," as He has brought me to this state to free me from yet another area of painful captivity. Maybe it is His way of freeing me of the frog in my throat as I share my faith and writings to help others become free in Him as well. I don't know. I still have a lot to learn, but I do know that the truth will set us free.

Truth is found in the Bible and by walking in the spirit (the light of God with Jesus as our model). Psalms 139 states that "the darkness is as light to God," so even in darkness we cannot escape Him. He holds us in His arms. He catches us when we fall. He alone never fails us. I have a heart for the suffering of those in captivity. But more importantly, God has a heart for those in captivity, those enslaved by whatever their Egypt is, those fighting to place their faith in Him. Is there a frog in your throat? There was in mine. We need to fully rely on God, our awesome, heavenly Father, who is waiting and wanting to set us free. At first I could not share my testimony because of my own sense of imprisonment and captivity. I was afraid to speak out. I lacked my own ability to demonstrate consistent faith. But God has set me free. We need to build a relationship with Him with focus, intimacy, obedience, prayer, Bible reading, songs of praise and Christian fellowship. We need to let Jesus help us with the bridge that He already built when He took our sins to the cross. He won't hurt us, rather He will make us whole. We need to reach out to Him and touch His cloak. Our faith in Him will heal us and set us free. I say to us now as He said to the woman in Mark 5, "Go in peace and be freed from your suffering." Hallelujah! Amen.

The Authority Invested In Me

Sharing with conviction and boldness is what I believe God wants of me as I write prayerfully, openly, honestly, thoughtfully with the authority He provides and through the credibility of experience. While I search the Bible and ground my experiences in the truth of God's Word, I'm not interested in imposing what I've shared upon anyone. I'm mostly interested in sharing in a way that what I share will help someone else. The insight God gives me illustrates the vast difference between what is of me and what is of Him and His Word. I am so little and pitiful next to Him.

During a trip to Tennessee with some friends, God showed me the difference between when my sharing was from His anointing and when it was from my own desire to advise. I can't take myself totally out of this writing since it is so personal to my experience, so I ask you to only take what you need or what you feel that is God speaking through me to you.

What I am trying to say is that God is the final authority in your life and you must have faith to walk in His truth and His will. I believe He has given me the authority to share some things. If something written in the pages of these writings is for you, praise God! This book is about me, and yet it isn't. This book is about Him in me as much as I can die to myself and let Him have my life—trusting Him despite the outcome on this earth, trusting Him despite the persecution, trusting Him and receiving the joy of His love and faithfulness to me. He has a purpose for each of us even when it appears that He doesn't or when others seem to be against us.

In Genesis I am reminded of the awful things that happened to Joseph. His brothers were jealous of him because he was favored and plotted to kill Joseph. With the influence of one brother, they decided to strip Joseph of his special robe and throw him into a well. Then they sold Joseph into slavery and let their father think he had died. As a slave, Joseph became falsely accused of rape by his master's wife and was thrown into jail. Joseph could surely have felt abandoned by God by now and given up on their relationship, but he remained faithful.

God gave Joseph insight into the dreams of Pharaoh, and Pharaoh told Joseph, "Since God has made all this known to you, there is no one so discerning and wise as you. You shall be in charge of my palace, and all my people are to submit to your orders. Only with respect to the throne will I be greater than you" (Genesis 41:39-40). There was a seven-year famine in the land (which Pharaoh had prepared for due to the insights into the dreams). Joseph's brothers traveled to Egypt for food and in the end bowed down to Joseph. The family was reunited. After Joseph's father, Jacob, died, the brothers became afraid that Joseph would seek revenge upon what they had done to him. But Joseph said, "Don't be afraid. Am I in the place of God? You intended to harm me, but God intended it for good to accomplish what is now being done, the saving of many lives" (Genesis 50:19-20 LAB).

As I recall the spiritual warfare and some of the ways in which I have felt persecuted throughout my journey, I think of my dad, as well as the first therapist, and I think of Joseph. Whatever intentions there were, I have been harmed, but, like Joseph, God has had and continues to have a plan and purpose for my life. Whether through these writings or in other ways, God promises me that He is making those evil things that have harmed me for the good, just like with Joseph. Those who have played me as if I were their instrument have, in spiritual eyes and in God's power, been God's instruments used to accomplish good as, once again, His strength is made perfect through our weakness. Once again, I declare the word of the Lord for those held captive. Let my people go!

CHAPTER 12

After Birth

Many people add an Afterword to their writings, but how is it that I have a gentle prompting to write something about After Birth? And what is after birth supposed to be about anyway? After birth could have something to do with after having been reborn, but why is it that I keep seeing a picture in my head of the afterbirth that is delivered as a normal part of the delivery experience?

I began my writings in 1984 with Urgent Birth, so why not an after birth ending? In the Urgent Birth "poem," I talked about an erupting volcanic urge to express what could no longer be contained—that being, the child within. There ended up being a lot of "stuff" within and much to be birthed. So, maybe the after birth has something to do with working therapeutically through all this "stuff" that seemed like splitting me into parts to get all the memories and feelings out.

161

According to Hartman, C. R. & Burgess, A. W., in *Treating Incest; A Multimodal Systems Perspective,* (Trepper & Barrett, Eds., 1986):

> Dissociation from the sexual abuse appears to be a prime and immediate method used by children to survive sexual assault during the abuse phase. Survival behaviors manifested by child victims during sexual assault include complying; negotiating; fighting; experiencing amnesia; crying; freezing in terror; and actively pretending to be somewhere or someone else. We define dissociation as a general process in which the mind fragments psychic integrity in the service of survival. In other words, the child victim diverts mental attention away from the abuse. Dissociation is a normal reaction to an emotionally loaded situation (p.88).

The best and most simplistic way I know to describe the splitting is like a record album where there is a lead into each song. It's like the same vocalist with various background voices and instruments that makes each song unique. This time, the vocalist moves from song to song. She dances with the gravity of a quiet, private space between songs that pull her in. That "inner space" often contains no clear memory of the other songs. So, the vocalist emerges and responds to the song at hand, not always knowing how to respond, yet somehow sensing the expectation to carry on. She usually pulls the song off with a brilliant system of organization that allows the vocalist to survive the circumstances at hand.

Dissociation, rather than a sickness and far greater than a psychological diagnosis, is a brilliant coping mechanism that the person uses to survive a trauma that is far too huge to put one's mind around. This phenomenon is not all that unlike the numbness that accompanies a physical trauma to the body. This "gift" in coping, while it has its own challenges within the healing process, needs to be held in the positive light of which it truly is. There are those in the church who would see this means of coping as being demon possessed. There were demon-possessed people in the Bible, and Jesus and the disciples did cast out demons and bring healing to those who believed, but as the church we need to be careful not to bring more harm to God's children. We need to keep our focus on God's goodness and provision. Ultimately, He is the creator as well as the healer and deliverer. Surely, He is capable of creating a way for our minds to handle trauma.

While having lunch with a very special friend who understands something about what I had been through with this idea, I had the opportunity to think once again about them. I don't know whether these parts were there all along since sometime in childhood. I do think that some of the therapeutic "blunders" along the way caused further need of them. So, for anyone who understands what I am talking about, the difference between me and the infamous Sybil (that story being fact or fiction), is that I always know what I am doing. Therefore, to go back to my record album metaphor, I am aware of each song on my album. The thing is that I still go into the inner space (for me, a still and holy place. This is, on some level, a very normal experience—similar to people becoming dazed as they drive home from work on automatic pilot, for example).

I remember first going inside and exploring these parts of me. It was as though there was a funnel in which I spiraled downward while these hands kept reaching out to me. They were crying out for help. They needed to be heard. It was as if I had repressed thoughts and feelings throughout various ages of my life that were begging to be free. Now that I have shared these experiences, I imagine there are going to be those who judge or misjudge, those who psychologize or dehumanize, and those who just don't have a clue. My best advice is if you don't know what I'm talking about, don't worry about it. If you do know from personal experience, don't clutter your thoughts and life with those people who don't understand or who judge and misjudge, especially if they lack sensitivity. You have enough to sort through without coping with their stuff, too. I recommend sharing with someone who can handle what you are going through in a more delicate manner—even if not getting to communicate what is going on in your life with loved ones and receive their care feels like the kind of behavior that caused the splitting and repressed thoughts and feelings to begin with. This is obviously not society's everyday topic of conversation and carries with it a similar silence and stigma of incest. You can disagree, but to me it is one of those "forgive them for they do not know what they do things."

Again, if a loved one doesn't understand, I hope they don't ever have to know all of the dynamics of these things. My wholeness is in God alone. Someone observing me with a therapeutic eye or with knowledge of what I'm talking about may see various parts to me; however, "all of me" is plugged into my relationship with God. By the way, God is our heavenly Father, Jesus, and the Holy Spirit—three in one—-and I am made whole in Him.

In the video that accompanies her book, *Breaking Free; Making Liberty in Christ a Reality in Life*, Beth Moore states, "You do not have a truth that God's truth cannot overcome." I believe this statement wholeheartedly and that it is applicable to everything even including dissociation.

Now, to focus on distinguishing anything distinctly with regard to my personality only confuses me. I feel that focusing in that way causes a spiritual battle at this point because rather than enhance my relationship with God, it tries to bring about a separation from Him. Beginning with Adam and Eve in the Bible, we know that God does not want us to separate from Him. Still, for a "minute," the therapeutic work with dissociation was necessary, but people need to know that any diagnosis—medical or psychological—is not the final word.

In relationship to God having the final word, I am going to risk saying something else in this writing that in human eyes will appear like something other than what it is in spiritual eyes. I saw Jesus in a spiritual form three times on three separate snow-covered hillsides not so long ago. The message I received is how very present He is in my life. The funny thing is (once those of you who are purely scientific unbelievers, or are totally skeptical get past seeing me as delusional or having had a delusion on these three occasions), I tried to force myself to "imagine" Jesus beside me in my car as I was driving down the road. The attempt to imagine or create the image I had seen was wrong in two ways: 1.) It's all about His will, not mine; and 2.) Jesus doesn't want to be in any passenger seat! He wants to be the driver in my life (smile)! One person told me that what I saw was the power of suggestion, but each time I felt the

Holy Spirit upon me first. Then I looked to see what God was showing me. As I consider what happened, I believe that God was giving me a second message. Not only is He with me, but also I am not to allow science, unbelievers, or psychology to cause me to doubt His presence. I am not to doubt the supernatural power and ability to heal that God has in my life!

The third time I saw Him, I lowered my head and felt humbled. I sense that my feelings at that point were similar to Peter's with regard to what Jesus said in their conversation before ascending to heaven. Peter had denied knowing Jesus three times before the Savior's crucifixion. Three times after His resurrection, Jesus asked Peter, "Do you love me?" Each time when Peter responded affirmatively, Jesus replied, "If you love me, you will feed my sheep." I didn't make this connection until months later as I was reading my Bible. I also did not understand how important things in three are until later when the pastor's wife talked about the importance God puts on something when it happens three times such as saying, "Holy, Holy, Holy." While it would be safer not to talk about what I saw on those snow-covered hillsides, I believe I am not to keep this information to myself. I am to share it because if I love Jesus, I will feed His sheep.

With sexual abuse and dissociation, there truly is a dark place, but I also know that darkness is as light to God. I believe that how we experience this kind of trauma is similar to the way our body numbs itself when there has been a physical blow to it or like a shock response when there has been an emotional blow that is beyond our current ability to absorb all at once—such as a death of a loved one. I believe that these responses, like with being in a dissociative state, are gifts from our heavenly Father. When I have been in a dissociative place, I am well aware of God's love for me and I am also aware of my need to connect and remain whole in Him. Further, if I believe that God created a beautifully brilliant coping system for that which is meant to kill, steal and destroy so that we (His children who have been abused in such a devastating way) may live in Him, then He can also create the deliverance and bring to us abundant life as He heals His children beyond that brilliant system when it is no longer needed to survive.

Therefore, "love the Lord your God with all your heart, mind, soul, and strength, and love others as yourself. Live and "walk by faith, not by sight" (2 Corinthians 5:7 LAB). Also, in 2 Corinthians 4:16-18, it says not to lose heart. "Though outwardly we are wasting away, inwardly we are being renewed day by day. For our light and momentary troubles are achieving for us an eternal glory that far outweighs them all. So we fix our eyes not on what is seen, but on what is unseen. For what is seen is temporary, but what is unseen is eternal" (LAB). I pray that God continues to reveal Himself to you deeper and deeper each day as you continue this journey with Him. All to His glory and in His unfailing love.

Afterword

There is still pain sometimes as God will always be doing a work in me. Not unlike Jesus in Hebrews 5:7 (LAB), I will continue at times to "offer up prayers and petitions with loud cries and tears" as I submit to God in obedience. But what I have learned is that when I feel the lingering pain from something or someone, there is at least a moment that I must be thankful to the heavenly Father, knowing that He will help me embrace that pain and bring to me the gift of His healing touch upon my life. I don't even have to figure it out. I only have to keep my eyes on Him. Through all of the worship, Bible study, prayer, praise, and in searching elsewhere, there is still only one single conclusion: But for the grace of God, I am a lost soul. We all are.

How easy it is in a lowly position to lose sight of that. How easy it would be in a whirlwind of success to lose our way—like God's beloved David who had an affair with Bathsheba or like the Israelites' disobedience in the desert after their deliverance from the slavery of Egypt. There are certainly consequences, but God remains faithful in the cycle of human sin to keep His covenant of love with us. He is a most gracious and awesome God who offered His own Son, our Savior, Jesus Christ. There is no limit to God's grace, but there is a beginning each time we stop, confess our inability to be without Him, turn from our sins and toward Him, and receive His most glorious gift of grace—all free of charge. Without Him, I am a lost soul, you are a lost soul—we all are, but by grace we are saved.

Ask Him into your heart today if you haven't done so before. Surrender to Him right now. Let Him set you free. There is a

Promised Land, but in this world, there is also a fictitious place of peace and happiness forever after. We see glimpses of God's glory, and experience freedom through Jesus, but freedom doesn't mean that all of life is without imperfections. Freedom doesn't mean that you must walk around like a robot comparing your insides to other people's outsides and being sure you are "looking at the cup half full." Rather freedom encompasses opening the door of one's heart and letting Jesus in through all things. There are memories and present-day circumstances that hurt us and cause sadness. Our experiences are part of our testimony in which we turn loose (like with this writing), for God to use for His purposes as we run to Him with everything. Sometimes, the cup is simply half empty as we see Jesus hanging on the cross, yet there is a positive choice to be made when we also see Him as the Risen Savior.

God provides salvation and healing that fills the gaping holes in our lives! He offers freedom beyond what any of us can imagine. God has dreams for us beyond our wildest dreams. Surrendering our hearts in prayer, including asking God to take what we cannot release on our own, opens our hearts to the heavenly aerodynamics of spiritually flying above our circumstances with Jesus. Choosing Him is the kind of positive living that rises above and transforms us beyond being computer-like beings. We fight to hide our hearts as we announce to the world what they think they want to hear—that we see the cup half full—and comparing ourselves to others who claim for themselves that they can see it that way as they search fruitlessly for power within themselves. God is the only power that fully completes and uplifts us. He alone is our source of hope. He Is the only One able to set us free.

If you haven't already, I pray that you will receive Jesus now and begin your own spiritual journey by giving Him all of the praise. Christ is Risen! Hallelujah! God is victorious and forever more will be!

> Dear merciful, heavenly Father, thank You for Your presence. Oh most Holy Spirit, I feel You as well as the joy of the work You are doing. Glory be to God! Praise God! Thank You! Thank You, Jesus! You are so good! In the end, we are all simply Your children. As I look back, I realize that nothing else matters. Thank You for the happy memories with the people who I have referred to in the pages of this writing— especially for the joyous times when we were simply and solely Your children together. Those times and the memories of them are beautifully made by Your hands, awesome Creator, my heavenly Father. In Your name I pray, Lord Jesus, our Savior. To your glory, I commit these works. Hallelujah! Amen

Special Thoughts

My "Little Girls"

A rose is a creation of beauty, a symbol of love. As with all things, the life of a rose begins and ends. But the love that it represents lives on forever. As does my love for you.

My Marriage

We join together and we are one. Every part of our bodies embrace. You reach into me and touch my heart. I look into your eyes and see your soul. In time, our bodies separate and you are still in my heart, and we are still one. . .I love you.

My Mother's Love

Perseverance, patience and warm tea when I'm sick. Hugs, I love you, German chocolate cake, laughter and wit.

The birth of my own daughters, the newness of knowledge, the love needed to stand still in their struggle to grow within and beyond a bond so complex with voids only God can fill. Seeing my mother's love standing the test of time, the search down long, narrow roads, the blame and the shame. My mother's love real and rich, steady and mine.

Ode to a Country Boy

Just a little boy runnin' 'round a country town, learned to play the guitar, made a country kind of sound. He learned to love the women, married one and settled down. Kept a picture of another, he still liked to run around. He played guitar in the morning, guitar in the night. He made love where he could, yet something wasn't right. He and his bride made seven children. There are more to be found, from a country guitar man makin' country all around.

Chorus: Ya gotta watch those fine lines. Don't cross those fine lines. Lord, watch those fine lines go flyin' by. Oh, watch those fine lines. Don't cross those fine lines. Lord, stop those fine lines gone flyin' by.

A gifted man guitar in hand, got to help inspire a country family band. Theirs was the family he wanted. Ours the one he had. Theirs lived out his dreams. Ours just made him sad. So, I started singin' in the church choir, singin' at the school, singin' on a record album; I was a singin' fool. Taught myself some guitar. Never got the country sound. They got the best of him. We got the rest. Those were the good times.

Chorus: Ya gotta watch those fine lines. Don't cross those fine lines. Lord, watch those fine lines go flyin' by. Oh, watch those fine lines. Don't cross those fine lines. Lord, stop those fine lines gone flyin' by.

He took me to the mountains. He took me to their show. He took me to some places his little girl should never know. He died at 48—no more runnin' 'round the town. I busted up my guitar—no more need to make that sound. Years flew by, came to hear that country band, still sharin' country family love and praisin' a country man. And me; I sang a song or two, thinkin' how things come around. Watched his bride in the arms of another boy from that same ole country town.

Chorus: Ya gotta watch those fine lines. Don't cross those fine lines. Lord, watch those fine lines go flyin' by. Oh, watch those fine lines. Don't cross those fine lines. Lord, stop those fine lines gone flyin' by.

Another Mother's Love

Oh Holy Spirit, I feel so drunk with your power upon me! Look at the cross that hangs in the front of my sanctuary. It's empty; the Christ child has risen! I say "Christ child" as the youth pastor speaks about the birth in the manger. It is Christmas Eve; yet I see Your birth, I see Your cross, and I feel Your resurrection upon me. Fill me with Your joy, holy One in Three. I see Mary with the babe in her arms. What is she to do with this Son of God; her baby boy? What is she to do but care for His motherly needs and give Him up to the world where He hangs for all to see? Oh Blessed Mary, did you feel so blessed as you watched your baby boy hang nakedly before the crowds being crucified so undeservingly? Oh dear Mary, could you scream the anguished screams of a mother's heart—so connected to her son's pain and so helpless to prevent it? Oh Mary, and then those words from that beautiful Christ child you held safely and securely in your arms—hadn't it just been the other day? Oh how you must have longed to hold Him now. Oh how you must have longed to destroy His murderers when out of the mouth of your little baby boy, the Christ child, the King of kings, came these words, "Father, forgive them for they know not what they do." In your darkest moment, when did your heart melt blessed mother of the Risen Savior, mother of that babe in your arms on that blessed starry night? Was it the moment of our gift of eternal life? Was it then that you forgave us too? Oh God, our heavenly Father, thank You for Your forgiveness and for the heart of a mother's love. In Jesus' name. Amen.

Beyond The Glass (Grace)

Beyond the glass, pure, untouchable,
white snow on a hillside where cloak
and garment house the hovering spirit
grace

Beyond the glass, pure, untouchable,
light flashes where water and cleansing
reveal the still lingering innocent
grace

Beyond the glass, pure, untouchable,
candlelight burning where hearts
and souls bond unwavering love
grace

Beyond the glass, pure, untouchable,
hungry hearts surround a meal where fatherly
and family pray for delivering sustenance
grace

Beyond the glass, pure, untouchable,
Christ child on a hillside where sin
and suffering transcend restoring freedom
grace

Beyond the glass, pure, untouchable,
blessed being on a bed where death
and life meet restful, comforting peace
grace

Beyond the glass, pure, untouchable,
tender arms embrace where parent
and child discover His heavenly home
grace

Beyond the glass, pure, untouchable,
hovering, lingering, unwavering, delivering,
recovering, comforting, Heavenly
grace

Beyond the glass (Grace).

ABOUT THE AUTHOR

Denise Stewart has earned a Master of Science degree in Student Personnel Administration with a specialization in counseling and student development. Her internships have included campus ministry and educational development counseling in higher education. Denise has a Bachelor of Science degree in Psychology and was a caseworker in foster care agencies for children and youth and with Big Brothers/Big Sisters.

Denise has also served as a treasurer for the Westmoreland Association of Volunteer Administrators and was active in the Westmoreland County Teen Pregnancy Prevention Coalition. Earlier in her career, Denise worked in retail management, volunteered as a crisis counselor, and served as a contact person for an adult survivors of childhood sexual abuse self-help group.

Denise has spent her life worshipping and serving God through numerous church-related ministries and activities. She has also been trained and served as a Stephen Minister. Denise and her husband, Jerry, travel often and especially enjoy time with their daughters, son-in-law and grandchildren.

**To contact Denise Stewart
or to place an order for Finding the Way:**
Visit her website: www.findingtheway.net
or write:
Denise Stewart
~~P.O. Box 864~~
~~Orchard Park, NY 14127~~